7 RIVALS
OF FAITH

CHRIS HARRIS

Dedication

In the Bible, James 1:27 says that pure and faultless religion in God's eyes is to look after orphans and widows in their distress and to keep oneself from being polluted by the world. This means that true religion is not just about outward practices, but about showing compassion to the vulnerable and living a life that reflects God's values. It includes justice, mercy, humility, and holiness. True religion is seen in how we treat others and how we keep our hearts clean before God. That said, I dedicate this book to my beautiful wife, Corrie, who strives to show Christ's love in everything she does.

"Corrie, thank you for the example of true religion you have set for me, our children, and everyone whose lives you have touched with your kindness and compassion. You are an inspiring woman—indeed."

With love and respect,

—*Chris Harris*

Table of Contents

Foreword

It was December 1995 when I first met Chris. He had driven 80 miles from Dallas to our home to discuss his intention to seriously date our daughter, Corrie. As parents of four daughters, we always appreciated a man who understood the importance of starting a relationship with us as he got to know our daughter better.

We had an active household at that time. Everyone was busy that Sunday afternoon, for his first visit. We had heard a lot of excitement about Chris from Corrie, who was also living in Dallas. I was in the kitchen making last-minute preparations when they arrived. As I turned to go and greet them, Chris rounded the corner. When I suddenly saw that tall young man, I knew that I knew he was "the one." And I was right. Less than three months later, they were married.

When my husband, Vernon, and I married in 1963, he was already a pastor. Since then, we have always been involved in some form of ministry. He has traveled to about nine countries, teaching pastors and leaders so they could, in turn, teach their people. He spent years developing Bible curriculum for Bible schools and prisons. If we had to choose a verse for our lives together, it would be, "O magnify the Lord with me, and let us exalt his name together!" (Psalm 34:3).

My faith walk began as a child wanting to know God and transformed into a personal relationship with Jesus when I was almost 20. It was then that the things I knew about God became alive and personal. Marrying a pastor and having a life of ministry was a natural progression. I've been a stay-at-home mom, taught school (both public and private), worked in the business arena, and am a certified life coach.

It was also a natural progression to want our daughters to marry strong Christians who would love and care for them and live their lives with integrity and honesty. That was Chris from the start, and almost 30 years later, as his mother-in-law, I see him continue to demonstrate those qualities.

He is a highly motivated man who works hard at whatever he does. His faith hasn't changed what he does—it has changed his "why." Whether he created safety inventions, developed his own version of martial arts, trained military special forces, wrote books, or motivated people as a keynote speaker to become their better selves, at the core has been his faith. It's the fuel to his fire.

A faith walk is a journey, not a destination. On the trail, there are times of great celebration. In the shadows, there can be times of great pain. When we are challenged about the goodness of God, or even if He truly cares, we have a choice to make, which is to trust God or walk away. They make us bitter, or they make us better. Chris has faced major challenges to his faith many times throughout the years. Some are deeply painful. He has met those rivals to his faith and says, "I've tried life without Jesus, and I've tried life with Him. Life is exceedingly better with Him."

—*Martha Hedge*

Introduction

I remember the first time I heard Mel Gibson's famous line in the movie Braveheart, in 1995, when he passionately said, "Every man dies, not every man truly lives." Those powerful words stirred my soul deeply, most likely due to the life-changing epiphany I had experienced just one year earlier when I made the decision to truly live by becoming a Christian.

Before my salvation experience, I knew pleasure, but I wanted joy. I had life, but I wanted eternal life with Him. I wanted to be free from the chains of unforgiveness I had carried around since childhood. I longed to know His peace—the peace that surpasses all understanding. The Good News: I could have it all for the price of repentance, belief, and acceptance.

Most tombstones engrave the date of birth and death, with a small dash in between. Through much introspection, I have learned that the dash in the middle is significantly more important than the numbers themselves. For some people, merely surviving until death is their dash, with self-preservation being their ultimate driver. For others, the dash may be their success, career, family, or a worthwhile cause.

For me, accepting Jesus as my Lord and Savior forever changed my life. From that day forward, I have been on a deliberate journey of continuous learning. Some of the lessons I've learned along the way were born of hard work and passionate effort, while others were learned from adversity and pain. Nonetheless, I'm excited to share my journey and lessons with you on the pages that follow.

—*Chris Harris / Author & Warrior for Christ*

RIVAL 1

---◆---

FEAR

"Walk in His Freedom"

Chapter One

God's Approval Beats Human Applause

Rival I: Fear

I n a world obsessed with image, reputation, and acceptance, one of the most paralyzing barriers to becoming a Christian isn't disbelief—it's the fear of being judged. Many feel a pull toward God, a stirring in their spirit, and a hunger for something more—but hesitate at the crossroads. Why? Because they're afraid of how others might see them. Afraid of being labeled "too religious," "naive," or "fanatical." But allowing the fear of human judgment to silence your spiritual conviction is one of the most tragic ways to miss out on the most important relationship you'll ever have—your relationship with Jesus Christ.

The Fear of Man Is a Trap

Proverbs 29:25 puts it plainly: *"The fear of man lays a snare, but whoever trusts in the Lord is safe."* Fear of judgment is a snare—it entangles your heart, delays your decisions, and chains your freedom. It tricks you into trading eternal purpose for temporary approval.

People often resist Christianity not because they don't believe, but because they're afraid of what others will say. They fear ridicule, rejection, or being viewed as "too extreme." This fear is amplified in a culture that glamorizes self-reliance and mocks faith as weakness or fantasy. But make no mistake: choosing to follow Jesus is not weakness—it is the greatest act of strength and surrender combined. It is bold, countercultural, and eternally wise.

Jesus Was Judged, Too—And Still Loved Boldly

If anyone understood the sting of being judged, it was Jesus Himself. He was called a blasphemer, a lunatic, a rebel, and a threat. His love and truth offended many. He was betrayed, mocked, and crucified—not because He did wrong, but because He did what was right in the face of religious and social pressure.

Jesus never promised that following Him would earn the world's applause. In fact, He warned us it wouldn't. *"If the world hates you, keep in mind that it hated me first"* (John 15:18). Choosing Jesus means choosing to live for an audience of One, even when it draws criticism from others.

You're Not Alone in Your Hesitation

Countless people, from teenagers in high schools to executives in boardrooms, struggle with this very tension—feeling drawn to Christ but fearing the fallout from friends, family, or peers. What will they say? What if they think I'm weird? What if I lose relationships?

But consider this: What if someone is willing to walk away from you because of your pursuit of truth, love, and salvation? Were they ever truly walking *with* you? Fear of being judged by others often exposes how much weight we place on their opinions—sometimes more than God's. But faith begins when we care more about *God's approval* than *human applause*.

Real Courage Is Following Conviction, Not Comfort

The greatest freedom you will ever experience is the moment you stop needing permission to follow God. Christianity is not about pleasing people—it's about being transformed by grace, rescued by truth, and set on a mission bigger than yourself.

God is not calling you to be perfect. He's calling you to be *His*. The journey of faith doesn't begin with impressing others, but begins with surrendering your fear and trusting in Jesus. It takes courage to say, "I'm no longer living for the opinions of the crowd—I'm living for the One who gave His life for mine."

Eternity Is Worth More Than Popularity

Jesus asked, *"What good is it for someone to gain the whole world, yet forfeit their soul?"* (Mark 8:36). When you delay responding to the call of Christ because of fear of others' opinions, you're gambling eternity for approval that won't last past this life. The opinions of people change with trends. The love of God is eternal.

Every time you silence your faith to avoid being judged, you miss an opportunity to walk in freedom. Every moment you wait to say yes to God is a moment spent under the weight of human expectations. But when you finally step out of that fear and say yes to Jesus, something shifts. Your identity becomes anchored in something immovable. And no critic, no mocker, and no doubter can take that from you.

Final Thoughts

Don't let fear rob you of your faith. Don't let the loud voices of a broken world drown out the whisper of the Holy Spirit calling you home. You were made for more than the shallow approval of man. You were created to walk in freedom, truth, and purpose through Jesus Christ. Say yes to Him—not because it's easy or popular—but because it's right, it's real, and it's worth it. Are you ready to stop fearing judgment and start living with purpose?

Taking Action

Think | Write | Grow

Based on what you learned in this chapter:

What's something you will stop doing or a habit you will break?

_____

_____

What's something you will start doing or a habit you will create?

_____

_____

What's the potential positive impact of improving in this area?

_____

_____

Chapter Two

Being in Control Is Only an Illusion

Rival I: Fear

O ne of the most common, yet unspoken, reasons people avoid becoming Christians isn't because they doubt God's existence—it's because they fear what faith might demand of them. Beneath the questions, hesitation, or even resistance lies a deeper struggle: the fear of surrendering control.

To follow Christ means handing over the steering wheel of your life. It means trusting in something bigger than yourself, giving up the illusion of total independence, and embracing a path where you are no longer the ultimate authority. That reality can feel threatening—especially in a world that glorifies self-determination and personal autonomy. But what many fail to realize is that the control we fight so hard to keep is the very thing keeping us from the peace, freedom, and purpose we desperately crave.

The Illusion of Control

Control is comforting—at least on the surface. We love the idea that we are the architects of our own destinies, that we can manage outcomes, protect ourselves from pain, and build lives entirely on our terms. But the truth is, control is often just an illusion. We cannot control the future. We cannot guarantee our health, our relationships, our careers, or even the next breath we take.

When we refuse to surrender to God out of fear of losing control, we are clinging to a lie—that we are safer trusting in ourselves than in our Creator. But self-reliance becomes a prison when it separates us from the One who sees the whole picture and holds eternity in His hands.

Surrender Is Not Defeat—It's the Beginning of Freedom

The word *surrender* can sound like weakness or failure. But in the context of faith, surrender is not defeat—it's a decision to stop striving, stop pretending, and stop carrying burdens you were never meant to bear alone. Jesus said in Matthew 11:28-30, *"Come to me, all you who are weary and burdened, and I will give you rest... For my yoke is easy and my burden is light."*

That rest, that peace, is only available through surrender. It's not about losing your identity—it's about discovering who you truly are in Christ. When you finally lay down your need to control everything, you make space for God to lead, heal, and transform you in ways you could never accomplish on your own.

Trusting the One Who's Already in Control

The irony is, we fear surrendering control to God, yet He's the only One who has real control in the first place. God is not asking for your surrender because He wants to dominate your life—He's asking because He wants to *redeem* your life. He knows where you're broken. He sees the storms ahead. He understands the purpose for which you were created. Trusting Him isn't blind—it's wise.

God's sovereignty isn't something to fear, but something to rest in. Psalm 46:10 reminds us, *"Be still, and know that I am God."* That stillness only comes when you stop clenching your fists and open your hands to His will.

Holding On Keeps You Stuck

The fear of losing control can feel like self-protection, but often it's self-sabotage. You stay stuck in cycles of anxiety, burnout, and uncertainty, all while God is inviting you into something greater. You may tell yourself, "I'm not ready," or "I'll follow God when I have my life together," but the truth is, no one ever has full control. Waiting until you feel "safe" to surrender is like waiting for the ocean to calm before you take a step of faith. Faith isn't about having control—it's about releasing it.

Jesus doesn't call us to clean ourselves up before coming to Him. He simply says, *"Follow me."* The surrender comes first, and the transformation follows.

The Cost of Clinging

The rich young ruler in Mark 10 approached Jesus with enthusiasm but walked away grieving. Why? Because he wasn't willing to surrender control over his possessions, priorities, and plans. He wanted eternal life, but on *his* terms. How many people today are doing the same? Desiring the promises of God without submitting to the authority of God?

The cost of following Jesus is high—but the cost of clinging to control is higher. You may gain temporary comfort, but you forfeit the eternal peace, joy, and purpose that only God can give.

Final Thoughts

Don't let the fear of losing control rob you of the life you were created to live. What feels like loss is actually gain. What feels like risk is actually rescue. Choosing Christ is not about giving up freedom—it's about finally experiencing it. It's not about living a small, limited life—it's about stepping into something bigger than you ever imagined. When you surrender your control, you're not falling—you're being caught. You're not giving up—you're being lifted up. So let go. Trust the One who made you, knows you, and loves you. Let today be the day you stop resisting and start receiving the life only Christ can offer. Are you ready to surrender—not out of fear, but out of faith?

Taking Action

Think | Write | Grow

B ased on what you learned in this chapter:

What's something you will stop doing or a habit you will break?

_____

_____

What's something you will start doing or a habit you will create?

_____

_____

What's the potential positive impact of improving in this area?

_____

_____

Chapter Three

Love and Mercy Are Part of the Deal

Rival 1: Fear

O ne of the most powerful, yet paralyzing, reasons many people avoid becoming Christians is the fear of being judged and condemned by God. Deep down, they know their lives aren't perfect. They carry guilt from past mistakes, shame from hidden struggles, or wounds from past experiences. The thought of standing before a holy and righteous God feels terrifying. Instead of drawing closer, they retreat—believing they'll never be "good enough" for God. But that fear, while understandable, is tragically misplaced.

Yes, God is holy. Yes, He is just. But He is also the author of mercy, compassion, and unconditional love. Avoiding God because of fear of condemnation is like avoiding a doctor because you're sick. The very One we run from is the only One who can heal, restore, and forgive.

Misunderstanding God's Judgment

Many view God as an angry judge, waiting to condemn every failure. This image keeps countless people in hiding. They think, "If God really sees everything, then there's no hope for me." But that's not the message of the Gospel. That's not the heart of Jesus.

John 3:17 says it clearly: *"For God did not send his Son into the world to condemn the world, but to save the world through him."* The mission of Christ was not to shame or destroy sinners—it was to rescue them. God's judgment is real, but it is not His starting point. His starting point is *love*. He doesn't rejoice in punishment. He longs to redeem.

God Already Knows—and Still Invites You

The truth is that God already knows your worst moments, your deepest regrets, and your darkest secrets. And yet, He still invites you in. You don't have to pretend with Him. You don't have to clean yourself up before you approach Him. Romans 5:8 reminds us, *"But God demonstrates His own love for us in this: While we were still sinners, Christ died for us."*

Let that sink in: While we were *still* sinners. Not after we had fixed our lives. Not after we had earned His love. He died for us while we were at our lowest. The cross is not a symbol of judgment against you—it's a declaration of love for you. It shows the lengths God went to *remove* condemnation, not enforce it.

Condemnation Is the Voice of the Enemy, Not the Voice of God

The fear of being condemned by God is often fueled more by shame than truth. Satan is called the "accuser" for a reason. He whispers, "You're too far gone. You're too broken. God will never accept someone like you." But the Word of God says the opposite.

Romans 8:1 is a promise every heart needs to hear: *"Therefore, there is now no condemnation for those who are in Christ Jesus."* If you belong to Him, you are not condemned—you are *covered* by His grace. God doesn't look at you through the lens of your failures. He looks at you through the blood of Jesus, which makes you clean, forgiven, and free.

Grace Doesn't Excuse Sin—It Overcomes It

Some people avoid God because they think Christianity is just about pointing out what's wrong with them. But true Christianity isn't about highlighting sin—it's about healing it. Yes, God is holy, and He calls us to repent. But He does so because He loves us too much to let us stay in what's destroying us.

Grace is not God ignoring sin. Grace is God overcoming sin for us—through Jesus. When you say yes to Christ, you're not signing up for a life of fear. You're stepping into a relationship where mercy triumphs over judgment.

Fear Pushes Us Away—But Love Draws Us In

Fear of judgment causes us to hide. But perfect love drives out fear (1 John 4:18). The more you understand the heart of God, the less you will run from Him and the more you will run *to* Him.

God is not standing with arms crossed, waiting to punish you. He is standing with arms open, ready to forgive, restore, and adopt you as His own. He doesn't want you crushed by shame. He wants you raised by grace.

Final Thoughts

Don't let the fear of judgment keep you from the One who came to save you from it. The enemy wants you to believe God's holiness is a threat—but in truth, it's your hope. His justice ensures wrongs will be made right. His mercy ensures that sinners like us can be forgiven. You don't have to be afraid of God's judgment when you're standing in the shadow of His cross. If you've been holding back, thinking you're too messed up for God, remember that the Gospel isn't about you getting it right. It's about Jesus already making it right. Come to Him—not because you're perfect, but because He is. Are you ready to stop running from condemnation and start walking in grace?

Taking Action

Think | Write | Grow

Based on what you learned in this chapter:

What's something you will stop doing or a habit you will break?

_____

_____

What's something you will start doing or a habit you will create?

_____

_____

What's the potential positive impact of improving in this area?

_____

_____

Chapter Four

Everyone Is Hurt and Disappointed

Rival I: Fear

For many people, the idea of becoming a Christian stirs up more than just questions of faith—it awakens a deep, personal fear of being hurt or disappointed. Some have seen hypocrisy in Christians. Others have prayed desperately only to feel silence. Some carry church wounds, betrayal from believers, or disappointment when life didn't turn out the way they thought it would. And so, they hesitate. They keep God at a distance—not because they don't believe in Him, but because they don't trust Him not to let them down.

This fear is real. It's raw. And it's far more common than most people admit. But while the pain is valid, the solution isn't to keep God at arm's length. It's to bring that pain to Him honestly and discover that His love is greater than the wounds others may have caused.

When People Fail, Don't Confuse Them with God

One of the most heartbreaking reasons people avoid Christianity is because of how they've been treated by *Christians*. Maybe they were judged, excluded, gossiped about, or abused by people who claimed to represent Christ. Maybe the church became a place of shame instead of a sanctuary. These experiences can leave deep scars, and understandably, many begin to associate the failure of people with the failure of God.

But the truth is that flawed people don't define a perfect God. Jesus never once said His followers would be flawless. In fact, He warned of wolves in sheep's clothing and false teachers who would misrepresent His name. The Bible is honest about human weakness—even among believers. But those failures don't reflect the heart of Christ. He is not the one who betrayed, rejected, or wounded you.

Jesus never condoned religious hypocrisy. He confronted it. He never turned away the brokenhearted. He welcomed them. So, if people have hurt you, let Jesus be the one who heals you—not the one you blame.

Disappointment With God Is Not the End of Faith

There's also a more personal kind of fear—the fear that God will disappoint *you*. You've seen prayers go unanswered. You've experienced loss, suffering, or seasons of silence. You've wondered, *If I give my life to God, what if He doesn't show up the way I need Him to?*

This fear is hard to admit, but crucial to face. It stems from the belief that surrendering to God means life will go the way you hope. And when it doesn't, the disappointment can feel like betrayal.

But God never promised a pain-free life—He promised *His presence* through the pain. He never promised to give you everything you want—but everything you *need* for your soul. Isaiah 55:8 reminds us, *"For my thoughts are not your thoughts, neither are your ways my ways,"* declares *the Lord.* This means God's plan might not always make sense in the moment—but it is always rooted in eternal wisdom and unshakable love.

Faith doesn't remove disappointment—it reframes it. It teaches you that even in the waiting, even in the heartbreak, God is working something deeper, truer, and more beautiful than you can imagine. He's not the cause of your pain. He's the healer in the middle of it.

Jesus Knows Your Wounds—And He Wants to Heal Them

Jesus isn't indifferent to your pain. He walked this earth, was betrayed by friends, rejected by His own people, and hung on a cross by the very ones He came to save. He knows what it's like to be hurt by others. He knows what it's like to cry out to the Father and hear silence.

You don't have to hide your fear or your disappointment from Him. He can handle your honesty. In fact, He invites it. In Matthew 11:28, He says, *"Come to me, all who are weary and burdened, and I will give you rest."*

You're not weak for being afraid. But you will remain burdened if you carry that fear alone. Let Jesus carry it. Let Him prove to you that He is not like those who have hurt you. His love doesn't fail. His character doesn't change. His grace doesn't run out.

Final Thoughts

Avoiding God because of fear of being hurt or disappointed is like staying in the dark because someone once misused the light. The failure of people, even in the church, is real—but it doesn't diminish the faithfulness of God. And your past pain, no matter how deep, doesn't disqualify you from experiencing the peace, love, and healing that only Christ can bring. Don't let fear of hurt keep you from the one relationship that can truly heal your heart. Don't let past disappointments rob you of future hope. Jesus isn't asking you to trust Christians. He's asking you to trust *Him*. And He will never fail you. Are you ready to stop holding back and finally let Jesus show you who He really is?

Taking Action

Think | Write | Grow

Based on what you learned in this chapter:

What's something you will stop doing or a habit you will break?

_____

_____

What's something you will start doing or a habit you will create?

_____

_____

What's the potential positive impact of improving in this area?

_____

_____

Chapter Five

Sacrifice Leads to Greater Rewards

Rival I: Fear

For some, the hesitation to become a Christian isn't about doubting God's existence—it's about fearing what it might cost. What if following Jesus means I have to give up everything I enjoy? What if it means sacrificing my freedom, fun, or comfort? There's a widespread belief that Christianity is the end of personal pleasure, ambition, or self-expression. That to follow Jesus means living a life of restriction and denial.

But this perspective misses the heart of what it means to walk with Christ. Yes, following Jesus comes with sacrifice. Yes, it means turning away from certain desires, habits, or priorities. But what the world calls "sacrifice," heaven calls *exchange*—trading temporary gratification for lasting joy, empty pleasures for deep purpose, and self-centered living for a life anchored in love, freedom, and eternal fulfillment.

The Fear of Losing Pleasure Is a Shallow View of Life

In a culture driven by instant gratification, we're taught that the highest goal is personal happiness and pleasure. The problem is, most of what the world offers doesn't satisfy for long. The parties end. The relationships fail. The money doesn't fulfill. The attention fades. Still, many fear that becoming a Christian means forfeiting what little pleasure they do have.

But Jesus never came to rob us of life. He came to give it—*real* life. In John 10:10, He says, *"I have come that they may have life, and have it to the full."* The pleasures God asks us to surrender are not because He's trying to limit us, but because He knows what will ultimately destroy us.

Sacrifice Isn't Loss—It's Gain

Every meaningful pursuit in life comes with sacrifice. Athletes sacrifice comfort to compete. Entrepreneurs sacrifice sleep to build their vision. Parents sacrifice time and energy for their children. So, why is it that when it comes to God, we expect everything to come without cost?

Jesus was upfront about what it means to follow Him: *"If anyone wants to come after me, let him deny himself, take up his cross daily, and follow me"* (Luke 9:23). But He didn't say that to scare us. He said it to show us that the path to something greater always passes through surrender. Following Christ may cost you something, but not following Him will cost you far more.

What you give up is nothing compared to what you gain—peace that passes understanding, purpose beyond this life, freedom from guilt and shame, and a love that never fails. Those who fear the sacrifice often forget the reward.

God Doesn't Ask You to Give Up Pleasure—He Redirects It

God isn't against pleasure. He created it. He gave us beauty, intimacy, creativity, laughter, music, and nature—all to be enjoyed. But He also gave us boundaries, not to steal joy, but to protect it. Like a fire in a fireplace, pleasure within God's design warms the soul. Outside of it, it burns everything down.

When God asks you to lay something down, it's not because He's trying to rob you—it's because He's trying to restore you. Sin promises pleasure, but delivers pain. It thrills for a moment, then enslaves. Jesus doesn't offer counterfeit happiness—He offers *abundant life*. Real joy. Real freedom.

You're Not Alone in the Process

Another common fear is that once you become a Christian, you'll have to become someone you're not—overnight. That you'll instantly have to cut ties with everything and everyone in your life. But transformation in Christ is a *process*, not a performance. God meets you where you are and walks with you as He reshapes your desires and gives you the strength to surrender what's holding you back.

It's not about behavior modification—it's about heart transformation. And that transformation doesn't come through willpower, but through grace. Philippians 2:13 says, *"For it is God who works in you to will and to act according to His good purpose."*

One of the biggest lies in our culture is that freedom means doing whatever feels good. But real freedom isn't the absence of boundaries—it's the presence of purpose. Without God, we end up mastered by our own desires. We chase after what feels good in the moment, only to wake up feeling empty, guilty, or lost.

Jesus sets us free—not to indulge the flesh, but to live with meaning, clarity, and joy. Galatians 5:1 says, *"It is for freedom that Christ has set us free."* The Christian life isn't about giving up pleasure—it's about discovering deeper, lasting joy rooted in truth.

Final Thoughts

Don't let the fear of personal sacrifice keep you from the greatest relationship you'll ever know. Yes, following Jesus means laying some things down. But in return, you gain what the world can never offer—peace with God, joy in your soul, and eternal life through grace. Whatever you're afraid of losing is nothing compared to what you're being invited to receive. Don't settle for temporary satisfaction when God is offering you eternal significance. Are you ready to stop fearing what you'll give up and start embracing what you'll gain?

Taking Action

Think | Write | Grow

Based on what you learned in this chapter:

What's something you will stop doing or a habit you will break?

_____

_____

What's something you will start doing or a habit you will create?

_____

_____

What's the potential positive impact of improving in this area?

_____

_____

Chapter Six

It's Far Better to Fail Than Not Try

Rival 1: Fear

The hesitation to become a Christian doesn't always come from a lack of belief in God—it sometimes comes from a deep, lingering fear of not measuring up. Not to God, necessarily, but to other *Christians*. The fear sounds like this: *What if I'm not good enough? What if I don't know the Bible like they do? What if I mess up? What if they judge me because I'm not like them?*

This fear creates a false but powerful narrative that Christianity is only for the perfect, the polished, or the already holy. It whispers that unless you can meet certain spiritual standards, walk a certain way, or speak in religious language, you don't belong. That lie keeps countless people from stepping into the grace of God—not because He is pushing them away, but because they feel pushed away by the pressure of others' expectations. But that's not the Gospel. That's not Jesus. And that's not how true Christianity works.

God Doesn't Start with Perfection—He Starts with Surrender

If Christianity were only for the perfect, then no one would qualify. The very heart of the Gospel is that *no one* measures up on their own. Romans 3:23 makes it clear: *"For all have sinned and fall short of the glory of God."* That includes everyone—from the lifelong churchgoer to the person just beginning to explore faith.

God doesn't wait for you to clean yourself up before He accepts you. He meets you in your mess, your doubt, and your brokenness. He starts with *grace*, not grading. Becoming a Christian is not about meeting human standards—it's about receiving divine mercy. It's not about proving yourself to others—it's about trusting in the One who gave everything for you.

Jesus Rebuked the "Religious Elite" More Than the Broken

Throughout the Gospels, Jesus consistently welcomed the outcasts, the sinners, and the spiritually unqualified. But He had strong words for the Pharisees—the religious leaders who burdened others with impossible expectations while boasting about their own righteousness.

In Matthew 23:4, Jesus says of them: *"They tie up heavy, cumbersome loads and put them on other people's shoulders, but they themselves are not willing to lift a finger to move them."* That same spirit still exists today when Christians care more about image, rules, and religious appearances than about love, compassion, and grace.

If you've been turned off by Christians who act superior, rigid, or condemning, remember that they do not represent the full heart of Christ. Jesus didn't come to build a religious club—He came to build a family of the forgiven.

You're Not Called to Meet *Their* Standards—You're Called to Follow *His* Voice

Too often, people delay saying yes to Jesus because they're intimidated by the perceived expectations of other Christians. They fear they won't pray "right," act "spiritual" enough, or know how to navigate church culture. But Christianity is not a performance for others—it's a relationship with God.

God isn't interested in religious rituals without heart. He's after *you*. He wants your honesty, your willingness, and your trust. He doesn't demand that you meet others' standards—He asks that you follow *Him*. That means your journey will look different from someone else's, and that's okay. God is not in the business of comparison. He's in the business of transformation—one heart at a time.

Spiritual Growth Is a Journey, Not a Competition

Becoming a Christian doesn't mean you suddenly have all the answers or will never struggle again. It means you begin a journey with Jesus—a journey of learning, growing, and becoming more like Him. There will be moments of strength and moments of weakness. Times when you feel confident and times when you fall short. But that's part of the process.

God is patient with you. Philippians 1:6 says, *"He who began a good work in you will carry it on to completion until the day of Christ Jesus."* You don't have to fake it. You don't have to rush it. You simply have to be willing to walk with Him, one step at a time.

The Church Should Be a Hospital, Not a Showcase

The church isn't supposed to be a display of perfect people—it's meant to be a place of healing for the broken. Sadly, not every church or Christian models this well. But don't let the failure of some believers cause you to miss the beauty of God's grace. The people in the church are the patients, not the physician. They're in need of grace, just like you.

When Christians put pressure on others to "look" holy instead of *becoming* holy through grace, they miss the point of the Gospel. And when you say yes to Jesus, you're not signing up to impress anyone—you're entering into a personal, transformative relationship with the Savior of your soul.

Final Thoughts

Don't let the fear of not measuring up keep you from the God who loves you beyond measure. You don't need to have it all together. You don't need to impress anyone. You just need to come as you are. God is not asking you to meet the expectations of others. He's asking you to trust Him, follow Him, and allow Him to shape you into who you were always meant to be. The journey begins not with perfection, but with a simple, courageous yes. Are you ready to stop fearing what others think—and start walking in the freedom of His grace?

Taking Action

Think | Write | Grow

Based on what you learned in this chapter:

What's something you will stop doing or a habit you will break?

_____

_____

What's something you will start doing or a habit you will create?

_____

_____

What's the potential positive impact of improving in this area?

_____

_____

Chapter Seven

Fear of the Unknown is Natural

Rival I: Fear

Fear of the unknown is one of the most powerful forces that holds people back—not just in life, but in matters of faith. For many, the hesitation to become a Christian doesn't stem from disbelief or rebellion, but from the uncertainty of what happens *after* the decision is made. What will change? Will I still be myself? What if I lose control over my life? What if God asks me to do something I'm not ready for?

This fear, though often unspoken, is very real. It's not just about theology—it's about identity, comfort, and the risk of stepping into unfamiliar territory. The fear says, *I don't know what this will cost me, so I'd rather stay where I am.* But what if the unknown you fear is actually the door to the life you were created to live?

The Call of Faith Always Includes Uncertainty

From the very beginning of the Bible, we see that following God has always required a willingness to walk into the unknown. God told Abraham, *"Go to the land I will show you."* He didn't give Abraham a map. He gave him a promise. The same is true for us. Christianity is not about having all the answers before you begin—it's about trusting the One who does.

Hebrews 11:1 says, *"Now faith is the substance of things hoped for, the evidence of things not seen."* In other words, faith begins where certainty ends. If you're waiting until everything makes perfect sense, you'll be waiting forever. The Christian life starts not with full understanding, but with full surrender.

You Don't Have to Know the Future—Just Trust the One Who Holds It

One reason people fear the unknown is because they're used to being in control. We make plans. We build routines. We protect our comfort zones. So, the idea of surrendering control to God—of letting someone else lead—feels risky. But here's the truth: You never really had full control to begin with.

Life can change in a moment. The job can end. The health report can shift. The relationship can fall apart. Control is an illusion. But God is not. He's the one constant in an unpredictable world. Choosing Him is not stepping into chaos—it's stepping into *security*. Jeremiah 29:11 reminds us, *"For I know the plans I have for you," declares the Lord, "plans to prosper you and not to harm you, plans to give you hope and a future."* The unknown may feel like a risk, but when God is leading, it's actually the safest place you could ever be.

God Calls You to Faith and to Follow

One of the biggest misconceptions about Christianity is that it demands blind faith. But faith in God is not blind—it's *trusting*. It's not irrational—it's relational. You may not know every step He'll ask you to take, but you can know *who* is asking. And that makes all the difference.

Jesus never promised a fully mapped-out life plan. But He did promise His presence: *"I am with you always, even to the end of the age"* (Matthew 28:20). That means even in the unknown, you are never alone.

God doesn't call you to figure it all out. He simply calls you to trust Him enough to take the next step.

The Unknown with God Is Better Than the Known Without Him

Staying in the familiar might feel safe—but if it keeps you from the life God has for you, it's not truly safe at all. The life you're holding onto may be predictable, but it might also be empty, chaotic, or without purpose. Jesus said, *"I have come that they may have life, and have it to the full"* (John 10:10). But you can't experience the fullness of that life if you're unwilling to leave your comfort zone.

Many of the greatest blessings in life are on the other side of uncertainty. Peace, purpose, healing, freedom, and forgiveness often come not when we stay in control—but when we let go and let God.

Final Thoughts

The fear of the unknown is real—but it doesn't have to rule your life. Don't let what you *don't* know about the future stop you from receiving what you *can* know about God: He is good, faithful, loving, and trustworthy. He isn't inviting you into confusion—He's inviting you into clarity, freedom, and eternal hope. You don't need to have it all figured out to say yes to Jesus. You just need enough courage to take that first step. And when you do, you'll discover that what once felt like the unknown is actually the beginning of everything you've been searching for. Are you ready to trust the One who already knows what's ahead—and loves you enough to walk with you through it?

Taking Action

Think | Write | Grow

Based on what you learned in this chapter:

What's something you will stop doing or a habit you will break?

_____

_____

What's something you will start doing or a habit you will create?

_____

_____

What's the potential positive impact of improving in this area?

_____

_____

RIVAL 2

— ◆ —

PRIDE

"Submit Yourself to God"

Chapter Eight

Wisdom Begins With Fearing the Lord

Rival 2: Pride

One of the most subtle yet powerful reasons many people avoid becoming Christians is not doubt, fear, or even rebellion—it's pride. Deep down, we don't want to admit that we need help. We don't want to confess that we are not enough on our own. We've built lives on self-reliance, reason, and personal achievement. So, when the idea of surrendering to God is introduced, it feels like weakness. It feels like failure. It feels like letting go of control.

But the truth is that refusing to admit we need God is not a sign of strength—it's a symptom of spiritual blindness. Relying on our own wisdom instead of God's might look impressive on the surface, but it always leads to emptiness, confusion, and brokenness beneath the surface.

The Trap of Self-Sufficiency

In today's world, independence is seen as a virtue. We are told to believe in ourselves, trust our instincts, and chart our own paths. And while personal responsibility and ambition have value, they become dangerous when they convince us that we don't need a Savior. Self-sufficiency becomes a wall that keeps God out.

Proverbs 3:5-7 warns us: *"Trust in the Lord with all your heart and lean not on your own understanding; in all your ways submit to Him, and He will make your paths straight. Do not be wise in your own eyes; fear the Lord and shun evil."* God doesn't say this to strip us of confidence—He says it to free us from the burden of pretending to be our own god.

Relying solely on human wisdom keeps us locked in cycles of frustration. We may experience success, but we often lack peace. We may have influence, but we still wrestle with purpose. The truth is, no matter how smart, talented, or resourceful we are, we cannot save ourselves. We cannot create meaning that satisfies the soul without the One who created the soul in the first place.

Pride Keeps Us From Grace

The core of the Gospel is this: *we need saving.* Not because we're weak in the worldly sense, but because we are sinful, limited, and in need of divine mercy. Admitting that we need God requires humility—and that's where many stop. Pride says, *I'm good enough on my own.* Pride says, *I'll come to God when I've fixed myself.* Pride says, *I don't need anyone to carry me—I'll carry myself.*

But James 4:6 reminds us, *"God opposes the proud but gives grace to the humble."* Pride blocks the flow of grace. Not because God withholds it, but because pride refuses to receive it. Grace can only fill the hands that are open—not the fists that are clenched in self-reliance.

Human Wisdom Has Limits—God's Wisdom Doesn't

There's nothing wrong with using the mind God gave us. But our understanding has limits. Our reasoning is shaped by personal biases, incomplete knowledge, and emotions. We only see a fragment of the bigger picture. But God sees it all—past, present, and future.

1 Corinthians 1:25 says, *"For the foolishness of God is wiser than human wisdom, and the weakness of God is stronger than human strength."* What this means is that even what seems simple or irrational by the world's standards—like surrendering your life to Christ—is infinitely wiser than trying to build a life apart from Him.

When we lean on our own understanding, we often chase success and still feel empty. We pursue pleasure and still feel restless. We gather knowledge, but still lack peace. God's wisdom is not just informational—it's transformational. It leads to peace, clarity, and eternal life.

The Strength in Surrender

Becoming a Christian is not about becoming weak—it's about becoming *whole.* It's not giving up your mind—it's giving God your heart. It's recognizing that the deepest strength is found not in independence, but in dependence on the One who designed you.

Surrender doesn't mean you stop thinking. It means you start *trusting*. It means acknowledging that God knows better, sees farther, and loves deeper than we ever could on our own. It's the beginning of true wisdom—because Proverbs 9:10 tells us, *"The fear of the Lord is the beginning of wisdom, and knowledge of the Holy One is understanding."*

Final Thoughts

Don't let pride rob you of purpose. Don't let the illusion of control keep you from true freedom. Don't let confidence in your own wisdom blind you to the beauty of God's truth. Admitting that you need God is not weakness—it's wisdom. It's not the end of your independence—it's the beginning of your identity. You were never meant to carry the weight of life alone. You don't have to have all the answers. You just need to know the One who does. Are you ready to stop relying on your own wisdom and start trusting the God who created you?

Taking Action

Think | Write | Grow

Based on what you learned in this chapter:

What's something you will stop doing or a habit you will break?

_____

_____

What's something you will start doing or a habit you will create?

_____

_____

What's the potential positive impact of improving in this area?

_____

_____

Chapter Nine

Our Wisdom Is Foolishness to God

Rival 2: Pride

I n a world that worships intelligence, degrees, innovation, and self-suf-ficiency, the idea that human wisdom could be considered foolishness seems almost offensive. We celebrate intellect and strategy. We applaud cleverness and cunning. We elevate reason and logic to the highest pedestal. But the Bible paints a very different picture—one that humbles the proud and silences the boastful: *"For the wisdom of this world is foolishness in God's sight"* (1 Corinthians 3:19).

This verse isn't a condemnation of thinking, learning, or studying. God created the human mind and delights in our pursuit of truth. But when human wisdom is used to reject or replace God—when it becomes an idol—we cross a dangerous line. We move from insight to arrogance. From brilliance to blindness. From knowledge to spiritual ignorance.

Human Wisdom Has Limits

We often forget that no matter how advanced our science, how brilliant our strategies, or how impressive our accomplishments, we are still finite beings. We only see a fragment of the entire picture. We draw conclusions from limited experiences. We chase meaning with minds clouded by pride, emotion, and self-interest.

God, on the other hand, sees the end from the beginning. He exists outside of time, beyond limitations, and with infinite understanding. Isaiah 55:8-9 reminds us of this clearly: *"'For my thoughts are not your thoughts, neither are your ways my ways,' declares the Lord. 'As the heavens are higher than the earth, so are my ways higher than your ways and my thoughts than your thoughts.'"*

Compared to God's wisdom, ours is a flicker in the dark.

The Cross: God's Wisdom That Confounds the World

Nowhere is the difference between God's wisdom and the world's wisdom more evident than in the message of the cross. To the world, the idea of a crucified Savior—God in human flesh, dying a brutal death for humanity's sin—sounds ridiculous. It doesn't make sense in terms of worldly logic or power. In fact, Paul addresses this directly in 1 Corinthians 1:18: *"For the message of the cross is foolishness to those who are perishing, but to us who are being* saved, *it is the power of God."*

This is the paradox of divine wisdom: what looks like weakness to the world—humility, sacrifice, surrender—is actually the very gateway to strength, redemption, and eternal life. The world tells us to seek self-promotion, but God calls us to humility. The world tells us to climb to the top, but God says the greatest among you will be the servant. The world says power is found in control, but God says power is made perfect in weakness.

When Wisdom Becomes an Idol

There's a difference between using wisdom and worshiping it. Many people today reject God not because they've searched for truth and found Him lacking, but because they've built a worldview on their own intellect—and anything that doesn't fit within their framework is dismissed.

This is why 1 Corinthians 1:27 tells us, *"But God chose the foolish things of the world to shame the wise; God chose the weak things of the world to shame the strong."* God often works through the unexpected—through the humble, the broken, and the surrendered—to reveal that His ways are not about human effort but divine grace.

When we elevate human wisdom above God's truth, we become wise in our own eyes and blind to the truth that sets us free.

True Wisdom Begins with Reverence

Proverbs 9:10 says, *"The fear of the Lord is the beginning of wisdom, and knowledge of the Holy One is understanding."* In other words, wisdom doesn't begin with intellect—it begins with humility. It begins with recognizing that God is God, and we are not. That His Word is truth, even when it challenges our opinions. That His commands are life, even when they confront our comfort.

True wisdom is not found in rejecting God, but in submitting to Him. It is the kind of wisdom that understands that faith, not pride, is the foundation of insight. That obedience, not arrogance, is the path to clarity.

Final Thoughts

God will applaud your intelligence, your logic, your success, and your self-reliance—but not if it is done independently of Him and leads you away from Him. Human wisdom that tries to navigate life without the Creator is not brilliance—it's blindness. It may shine for a moment, but it fades quickly in the light of God's eternal truth. Don't be fooled by the appearance of wisdom that has no foundation in God. Real wisdom bows in reverence. Real wisdom listens. Real wisdom leads to life. Are you ready to exchange the limitations of your own understanding for the limitless wisdom of God?

Taking Action

Think | Write | Grow

Based on what you learned in this chapter:

What's something you will stop doing or a habit you will break?

_____

_____

What's something you will start doing or a habit you will create?

_____

_____

What's the potential positive impact of improving in this area?

_____

_____

Chapter Ten

True Power Is the Result of Surrender

Rival 2: Pride

I n a world that glorifies independence, dominance, and self-made success, the idea that true power comes through *surrender* seems counterintuitive—if not offensive. We're taught that strength is found in control, that power is the ability to rule, and that the more we dominate life on our terms, the stronger we become. But God's Word presents a very different reality that teaches us that **true power isn't seized—it's received. And it only comes through surrender to the authority and Lordship of Jesus Christ.**

This is not a passive surrender or a defeatist mindset. It is the kind of surrender that unlocks supernatural strength, eternal authority, and unshakable purpose. It's the paradox of the Kingdom of God—when we kneel before Him, we rise with real power.

Surrender: The Gateway to God's Strength

One of the greatest truths in the Bible is that God's power is made perfect not in our control, but in our *weakness*. In 2 Corinthians 12:9, God says, *"My grace is sufficient for you, for my power is made perfect in weakness."* Paul responds not with protest, but with praise: *"Therefore I will boast all the more gladly about my weaknesses, so that Christ's power may rest on me."*

Why would Paul celebrate weakness? Because he understood a divine secret: when we stop trying to be our own source of power, we make room for *God* to be our source. His strength surpasses anything we could muster on our own. When we surrender our pride, our plans, and our self-reliance, God fills us with a power that is not dependent on circumstances, personality, or status—it's anchored in Him.

The Lordship of Christ: Not Just Savior, but King

Many people want Jesus as their *Savior*, but hesitate to embrace Him as *Lord*. But salvation and Lordship are inseparable. To follow Christ is not just to accept forgiveness—it is to yield to His authority. It means acknowledging that His way is higher, His Word is final, and His will takes priority over our preferences.

Romans 10:9 makes it clear: *"If you declare with your mouth, 'Jesus is Lord,' and believe in your heart that God raised Him from the dead, you will be saved."* This declaration is not a casual statement—it's a declaration of allegiance. To confess Jesus as Lord is to place every area of your life—your identity, decisions, relationships, finances, and future—under His care.

And here's the beauty of it: His Lordship is not oppressive; it is *liberating*. His leadership doesn't crush you—it lifts you. His authority doesn't diminish you—it completes you.

Surrender Is Not the End of Power—It's the Beginning

The world teaches that surrender is weakness, that to submit is to lose. But in the Kingdom of God, surrender is where true power begins. When you surrender to God:

- You gain **freedom** from the slavery of sin and shame.

- You receive **authority** to overcome spiritual battles.

- You walk with a **purpose** beyond your own ambition.

- You become a vessel of **divine influence**, not just human effort.

James 4:7 says, *"Submit yourselves, then, to God. Resist the devil, and he will flee from you."* Notice the sequence: submission comes before resistance. Authority in spiritual warfare doesn't begin with shouting at the enemy—it begins with surrender to God.

The Example of Jesus: Power Through Submission

Even Jesus, though fully God, modeled surrender. In the Garden of Gethsemane, facing the cross, He prayed, *"Not my will, but yours be done"* (Luke 22:42).

In that moment of ultimate surrender, the greatest act of power in history was set in motion—the redemption of humanity.

Philippians 2:8-9 says, *"He humbled himself by becoming obedient to death—even death on a cross! Therefore God exalted him to the highest place..."* Exaltation came *after* obedience. Power came *through* submission. Jesus didn't lose power by surrendering to the Father—He revealed what perfect power looks like.

Living Under His Lordship Releases Your Potential

When you truly surrender to the Lordship of Jesus, you're no longer driven by ego, fear, or comparison. You're led by conviction, guided by truth, and strengthened by grace. You stop living for approval and start living with *authority*. You are no longer just reacting to life—you are advancing the Kingdom of God.

Under His Lordship, you are protected, empowered, and aligned with a divine purpose. You become unshakable—not because of your strength, but because of His.

Final Thoughts

The world says, *"Take control to gain power."* God says, *"Give control to gain strength."* True power doesn't come from being self-made—it comes from being God-shaped. It's found not in grasping for more, but in letting go and letting Christ lead. Surrendering to God isn't the end of your strength—it's where your real strength begins. When Jesus is truly Lord of your life, you don't lose your identity—you discover it. You don't lose your power—you step into divine power that cannot be shaken. Are you ready to stop striving for control and start living in the power that only comes through surrender to the Lordship of Christ?

Taking Action

Think | Write | Grow

Based on what you learned in this chapter:

What's something you will stop doing or a habit you will break?

_____

_____

What's something you will start doing or a habit you will create?

_____

_____

What's the potential positive impact of improving in this area?

_____

_____

Chapter Eleven

Every Man Is Right in His Own Eyes

Rival 2: Pride

One of the greatest obstacles in our relationship with God is our refusal to admit when we're wrong. Refusal to acknowledge our failures, our sins, or our need for correction. Pride doesn't always roar—sometimes it whispers, *"I'm fine as I am."* But that stubborn refusal to repent or take responsibility is one of the most spiritually damaging postures a person can maintain. It hardens the heart, clouds our judgment, and—most importantly—*stifles our intimacy with God.*

God is not intimidated by our mistakes. He is merciful and eager to forgive. But what He cannot bless is a prideful heart that insists on its own righteousness while ignoring the truth. Our relationship with God doesn't thrive in perfection—it thrives in *humility, repentance,* and *truthfulness.*

Pride Builds Walls, Not Bridges

At the root of refusing to admit we're wrong is pride—a desire to protect our image, our ego, and our version of the truth. Pride resists correction. It justifies sin. It points fingers. And, most dangerously, it keeps us from approaching the throne of grace.

Psalm 138:6 reminds us, *"Though the Lord is exalted, he looks kindly on the lowly; though lofty, he sees them from afar."* In other words, God is close to the humble but distant from the proud. Not because He moves away from us, but because our pride moves us away from *Him.*

Just as pride ruins relationships with people—creating distance, silence, and resentment—it also erodes our connection with God. When we refuse to admit we've strayed, misjudged, or disobeyed, we resist the very grace that's meant to restore us.

Confession Is the Doorway to Renewal

God doesn't expect perfection. He expects *honesty*. 1 John 1:9 says, *"If we confess our sins, he is faithful and just and will forgive us our sins and purify us from all unrighteousness."* Notice the condition: *if we confess.* Forgiveness and restoration are always available—but they begin with *confession.* Admitting we are wrong isn't a spiritual defeat—it's a *spiritual breakthrough.*

King David, a man after God's own heart, made devastating mistakes. But what set him apart wasn't perfection—it was his willingness to repent. In Psalm 51, after his sin with Bathsheba, David cries out: *"Create in me a clean heart, O God, and renew a right spirit within me."* That humility reopened the path to intimacy with God.

Refusal to Admit Wrong Keeps Us Spiritually Stagnant

Some people wonder why their prayers feel ineffective, why their hearts feel dry, or why their relationship with God feels distant. Often, the root issue is unconfessed sin or unresolved pride. When we insist on being right—even when we're clearly wrong—we choose spiritual stagnation over growth.

Proverbs 28:13 warns, *"Whoever conceals their sins does not prosper, but the one who confesses and renounces them finds mercy."* God desires to pour out wisdom, guidance, and blessing—but He will not pour it into a proud, sealed heart.

Imagine a clogged pipe. The water is there, and the source is flowing, but nothing gets through because of a blockage. Pride is that spiritual blockage. Until we clear it through repentance, the flow of God's presence and power in our lives remains restricted.

Admitting We're Wrong Isn't Weakness—It's Wisdom

There's a cultural belief that admitting fault is weakness. That saying "I was wrong" is a sign of failure or shame. But in God's Kingdom, it's the exact opposite. Proverbs 9:8-9 tells us that a wise person *loves* correction and becomes wiser through it.

God isn't waiting for us to be flawless—He's waiting for us to be *honest*. A heart that is quick to repent, quick to listen, and quick to yield to God's truth is a heart that will grow in spiritual maturity and closeness with the Lord.

Relationships Require Honesty—and So Does Faith

No healthy relationship can survive without honesty. If we constantly deny fault, refuse correction, or pretend we're always right, we sabotage trust. The same is true in our relationship with God. He already knows the truth—what He wants is *for us to admit* it, *too.*

Jesus told a story in Luke 18 about a Pharisee and a tax collector praying in the temple. The Pharisee boasted about his righteousness; the tax collector simply said, *"God, have mercy on me, a sinner."* Jesus said it was the tax collector—not the proud religious man—who went home justified before God. Why? Because humility draws us near to the heart of God.

Final Thoughts

Our relationship with God is not hindered by our weakness, but by our unwillingness to *acknowledge* it. When we refuse to admit that we're wrong, we shut the door to healing, growth, and deeper intimacy with the One who longs to restore us. Admitting fault doesn't diminish our worth—it deepens our connection with God. It clears the air, breaks the chains of pride, and invites grace to flood in. Don't let pride keep you distant from the God who loves you. The freedom you're seeking is found on the other side of humility. Are you willing to open your heart, admit where you've gone wrong, and let God meet you with His restoring grace?

Taking Action

Think | Write | Grow

Based on what you learned in this chapter:

What's something you will stop doing or a habit you will break?

_____

_____

What's something you will start doing or a habit you will create?

_____

_____

What's the potential positive impact of improving in this area?

_____

_____

Chapter Twelve

Forgiving Others Is a Requirement

Rival 2: Pride

F orgiveness is one of the most powerful and transformative commands in the Christian faith. It lies at the heart of the Gospel and is the reason we can be made right with God through Christ. Yet, despite receiving God's grace, many believers still struggle to extend that grace to others. Whether it's because of deep wounds, repeated offenses, or personal pride, the refusal to forgive others for their mistakes, accidents, or poor choices doesn't just affect our relationships—it *damages our walk with God.*

Unforgiveness may feel like a form of control or self-protection, but in reality, it is a spiritual prison. It distorts our perspective, disrupts our peace, and ultimately hinders our relationship with the One who forgave us completely. When we withhold forgiveness, we don't just trap others in our bitterness—we trap *ourselves.*

Forgiveness Isn't Optional for the Christian Life

Jesus was clear and direct when He spoke about forgiveness. In Matthew 6:14-15, He says, *"For if you forgive other people when they sin against you, your heavenly Father will also forgive you. But if you do not forgive others their sins, your Father will not forgive your sins."*

These words aren't a suggestion. They are a command—and a warning. Forgiveness is not a feeling—it's an act of obedience. If we claim to follow Christ but refuse to forgive, we live in contradiction to the very grace that saved us. The cross didn't just pay for our sins—it set the example for how we are to treat others.

Unforgiveness Blocks God's Blessing

When we harbor unforgiveness, we create spiritual resistance in our lives. It's like holding onto poison and expecting it to hurt someone else. The bitterness, resentment, and anger we cling to become barriers to peace, joy, and spiritual growth.

Hebrews 12:15 warns us, *"See to it that no one falls short of the grace of God, and that no bitter root grows up to cause trouble and defile many."* That bitter root doesn't just affect one relationship—it infects our thoughts, our prayers, our worship, and even our witness.

We can't walk in the fullness of God's blessing while clinging to unforgiveness. God desires to pour out His favor, but He often waits for us to release what's poisoning our hearts.

Forgiveness Frees You, Not Just the Other Person

One of the biggest lies we believe is that forgiving someone means letting them off the hook or minimizing the hurt they caused. But forgiveness doesn't erase the past—it simply releases *you* from being chained to it.

Choosing to forgive is not saying the offense didn't matter—it's saying *your peace matters more.* It's recognizing that holding onto someone's debt won't bring healing, but letting it go will bring freedom.

Romans 12:19 reminds us, *"Do not take revenge...leave room for God's wrath."* When we forgive, we're not abandoning justice—we're entrusting it to the One who judges perfectly.

Unforgiveness Disrupts Unity in the Body of Christ

The Church is meant to be a place of grace, healing, and restoration. But when believers refuse to forgive one another, it fractures unity and invites division. Grudges between church members, resentment in families, and broken trust among friends weaken the Church's impact and testimony.

Jesus said in John 13:35, *"By this everyone will know that you are my disciples, if you love one another."* Love and unforgiveness cannot coexist. To reflect Christ, we must extend to others what He so freely gave to us.

Forgiving Doesn't Mean Forgetting—It Means Moving Forward

Some believers are hesitant to forgive because they assume it means reconciling with a toxic person or forgetting what happened. But forgiveness and reconciliation are not the same. Forgiveness is given; reconciliation is earned. You can forgive someone while maintaining healthy boundaries. You can release the offense while still guarding your heart.

Forgiveness is about *your freedom*, not about justifying their actions. It's about choosing to heal over hostility. It's about letting God deal with their choices while you walk in peace.

Final Thoughts

Unforgiveness is a heavy burden to carry. It drains your energy, clouds your spirit, and distances you from God's presence. As Christians, we are called to something higher—to love even when it's hard, to forgive even when it hurts, and to show grace even when it's undeserved. Why? Because that's exactly what God did for us. Don't let someone else's failure to become the chain that holds back your faith. Release the offense. Trust God with justice. And allow forgiveness to heal what bitterness could never fix. Are you ready to surrender your right to stay angry so you can step into the peace and power God has for you?

Taking Action

Think | Write | Grow

Based on what you learned in this chapter:

What's something you will stop doing or a habit you will break?

_____

_____

What's something you will start doing or a habit you will create?

_____

_____

What's the potential positive impact of improving in this area?

_____

_____

Chapter Thirteen

God's Grace Leads to Self-Forgiveness

Rival 2: Pride

One of the most overlooked, yet deeply destructive, struggles in the Christian walk is the inability—or unwillingness—to forgive *ourselves*. We may believe in God's mercy. We may even be quick to extend grace to others. But when it comes to our own mistakes, failures, or painful pasts—especially those things we didn't intend or couldn't control—we often hold ourselves hostage.

Whether it's a reckless decision, a missed opportunity, a painful accident, or a moment of weakness, many Christians walk around carrying guilt, shame, and regret like a heavy chain. And when we refuse to forgive ourselves, our spiritual life suffers. We may still go to church, read the Bible, and even pray—but deep down, we feel disqualified, disconnected, and defeated.

But that is not the life God has called us to. The Gospel doesn't just cover our sin—it frees us from *self-condemnation*. Refusing to forgive yourself doesn't honor God—it hinders Him from doing a full work in your heart.

You Were Not Meant to Carry What Christ Already Carried

The cross is not only about the forgiveness we extend to others—it's also about the forgiveness we *receive*. Romans 8:1 declares, *"Therefore, there is now no condemnation for those who are in Christ Jesus."* If Christ has forgiven you, why are you still condemning yourself?

When we refuse to forgive ourselves, we essentially say, *"The cross was enough for others, but not for me."* That's not humility—that's a distortion of grace. Jesus didn't die to give you partial forgiveness. He gave you *complete* freedom—freedom from guilt, from shame, and from the lies that say you'll never be whole again.

Self-Unforgiveness Paralyzes Purpose

Carrying guilt over past mistakes—especially those you can't change—will keep you stuck. It clouds your identity and silences your potential. You begin to believe you're unworthy to lead, serve, grow, or be used by God because of what you've done or failed to do.

But God specializes in redemption. Moses was a murderer. David was an adulterer. Peter denied Jesus. Yet each of them fulfilled powerful purposes *after* their greatest failures—because they embraced God's forgiveness. If you don't forgive yourself, you'll disqualify yourself from the very assignments God has already prepared for you.

God doesn't use perfect people—He uses *redeemed* people. Let Him redeem *you*.

Shame Is Not From God

There's a difference between conviction and condemnation. The Holy Spirit convicts us to bring us *closer* to God. Shame, however, drives us *away* from Him. Shame tells you that you're not enough, that your past defines you, that you'll never be free. But those are lies from the enemy—not the voice of your Savior.

Psalm 34:5 says, *"Those who look to Him are radiant; their faces are never covered with shame."* If God isn't ashamed of you, why are you ashamed of yourself? Shame chains us to the past, while grace launches us into the future.

Forgiving Yourself Doesn't Mean Forgetting—It Means Healing

Some people struggle to forgive themselves because they think it means pretending the pain didn't happen. But forgiveness doesn't erase your memory—it transforms your relationship with the memory. You may never forget what happened. But through Christ, the pain no longer defines you. The wound no longer controls you.

Isaiah 43:18-19 reminds us, *"Forget the former things; do not dwell on the past. See, I am doing a new thing!"* God wants to write a new story in your life, but you can't live it if you're stuck rereading the first chapters in regret.

Sometimes We Blame Ourselves for What Wasn't Our Fault

Another hidden form of self-unforgiveness comes from blaming ourselves for things outside our control—trauma, abuse, abandonment, or loss. Maybe it wasn't something you did, but something done *to* you. And somehow, you've internalized the belief that it was your fault. God wants to speak truth into that lie. You were not to blame. You are not responsible for the actions of others. And yet, you've carried shame as if you were. It's time to lay that burden down. God wants to heal *that* wound, too.

Final Thoughts

Refusing to forgive yourself does not make you more spiritual, responsible, or humble—it makes you a prisoner. It limits your faith, dims your joy, and undermines the power of the cross in your life. Jesus didn't just die to forgive you once. He died to forgive you *completely*. You are not your past mistake. You are not your worst moment. You are not what happened to you. You are a new creation in Christ. Forgive yourself—not because you deserve it, but because *He already paid for it*. Are you ready to lay down what you were never meant to carry and walk in the freedom Jesus died to give you?

Taking Action

Think | Write | Grow

Based on what you learned in this chapter:

What's something you will stop doing or a habit you will break?

_____

_____

What's something you will start doing or a habit you will create?

_____

_____

What's the potential positive impact of improving in this area?

_____

_____

Chapter Fourteen

Conquering Pride Is a Process

Rival 2: Pride

P ride is one of the most subtle and dangerous enemies of the Christian life. It hides behind our accomplishments, our opinions, and even our good intentions. Pride resists correction, craves attention, and convinces us that we are right even when we're not. In fact, pride was the root of Satan's fall and remains one of the most destructive forces in our relationship with God.

Proverbs 16:18 warns, *"Pride goes before destruction, a haughty spirit before a fall."* That's because pride blinds us to our need for grace, distances us from others, and hardens our hearts toward God. If left unchecked, it can destroy our witness, our worship, and our walk with Christ.

So, how do we conquer pride and walk in humility? Here are 7 biblical and practical ways to defeat pride and stay aligned with God's heart.

1. Remember Who God Is—and Who You Are Not

The first step to conquering pride is gaining a right view of God. When we truly see God's greatness, power, and holiness, we can't help but be humbled. Isaiah 40:15 says, *"Surely the nations are like a drop in a bucket; they are regarded as dust on the scales."* If the nations are a drop, what does that say about us? Humility isn't thinking less of yourself—it's thinking of yourself rightly in light of who God is. He is the Creator, and we are the created. He is infinite, and we are limited. When we keep that perspective, pride has no room to grow.

2. Embrace a Life of Prayer

Prayer acts as an antidote to pride because it acknowledges our need for God. When we pray regularly, we remind our hearts that we are not self-sufficient. Philippians 4:6 tells us to *"present your requests to God."* That act alone admits that we can't do life on our own. Consistent prayer cultivates humility. It teaches us to depend on God, listen to Him, and surrender control.

3. **Study and Submit to God's Word**

Pride thrives in ignorance and resistance, but it dies in the light of truth. Hebrews 4:12 says the Word of God is *"living and active... it judges the thoughts and attitudes of the heart."* When we regularly read and apply Scripture, it exposes our pride, corrects our thinking, and reshapes our character. Don't just read the Bible for knowledge—read it for transformation. Let it confront your ego and guide you into Christlike humility.

4. **Invite Correction and Accountability**

One of the marks of pride is defensiveness—an unwillingness to be corrected or challenged. But Proverbs 12:1 says, *"Whoever loves discipline loves knowledge, but whoever hates correction is stupid."* It doesn't get clearer than that. To conquer pride, we must welcome godly correction. Surround yourself with people who love you enough to speak the truth and listen with a teachable heart. Accountability helps guard against blind spots and keeps pride in check.

5. **Celebrate Others Without Comparing**

Pride constantly compares—it either elevates you above others or makes you feel threatened by their success. But Romans 12:15 encourages us to *"Rejoice with those who rejoice."* That requires a humble heart that isn't focused on self. When you learn to celebrate others' victories, talents, and blessings without needing to compete, you destroy pride's power and nurture a spirit of encouragement and unity.

6. **Serve Without Needing Recognition**

Pride craves applause. It wants to be seen, thanked, and admired. But Jesus modeled a radically different way—He *"did not come to be served, but to serve"* (Mark 10:45). When we serve quietly, without needing recognition or reward, we crucify our ego and become more like Christ. Practice anonymous generosity. Volunteer in hidden places. Do good when no one's watching. That's where humility is cultivated.

7. Focus on the Cross

At the cross, all pride must die. Why? Because it reminds us that we were so broken, Jesus had to die for us—yet so loved, He was willing to. The cross levels the playing field. No one is too good. No one is beyond grace. Galatians 6:14 says, *"May I never boast except in the cross of our Lord Jesus Christ."* When your identity is rooted in what Christ has done—not in what you do—you'll walk in humility, not pride.

Final Thoughts

Pride is sneaky. It doesn't always show up in arrogance or loud confidence—it often hides in subtle self-reliance, spiritual comparison, or the need to be right. But when we choose humility, we draw near to the heart of God. James 4:6 says, *"God opposes the proud but gives grace to the humble."* That grace empowers us to live free—free from comparison, control, and the pressure to prove ourselves. Conquering pride is not a one-time act—it's a daily surrender. But as we humble ourselves before God, we make room for His power, His peace, and His purpose to take root in our lives. Are you willing to lay down pride today so that Christ can be lifted up in you?

Taking Action

Think | Write | Grow

Based on what you learned in this chapter:

What's something you will stop doing or a habit you will break?

_____

_____

What's something you will start doing or a habit you will create?

_____

_____

What's the potential positive impact of improving in this area?

_____

_____

RIVAL 3

R E L I G I O N

"Relationship Over Ritual"

Chapter Fifteen

True Religion is Life-Giving

Rival 3: Religion

I n today's world, the word *religion* often carries mixed emotions. Some hear it and think of peace, purpose, and moral guidance. Others associate it with judgment, hypocrisy, or oppression. The truth is, not all religions are the same. The Bible itself speaks of both *pure* and *corrupt* religion. There is true religion that reflects God's heart—and there is man-centered religion that distorts it.

Understanding the difference between these two is essential for any Christian who desires to walk in truth, grace, and spiritual freedom. The goal is not to throw out religion altogether, but to reject the *man-centered systems* that misrepresent God while holding fast to the faith that draws us closer to Him.

Religion as God Designed It: Life-Giving and Transformative

Religion, in its purest, biblical form, is not a bad thing. James 1:27 tells us, *"Religion that God our Father accepts as pure and faultless is this: to look after orphans and widows in their distress and to keep oneself from being polluted by the world."*

This kind of true religion:

- Flows from a heart surrendered to God

- Produces compassion, mercy, and humility

- Anchors itself in the truth of Scripture

- Expresses faith through action, not just belief

- Keeps the focus on loving God and loving others

Healthy, God-centered religion provides structure for spiritual growth. It encourages prayer, worship, Scripture reading, fellowship, and service. It reminds us of God's holiness while inviting us into a relationship with Him. When guided by grace and truth, religion is a tool that supports, not suffocates.

Man-Centered Religion: A Counterfeit That Controls

On the other hand, man-centered religion is not rooted in God's heart—it's a human construct often shaped by pride, tradition, or the desire for control. Jesus confronted this directly in Matthew 15:9 when He said, *"They worship me in vain; their teachings are merely human rules."*

Man-centered religion tends to:

- Focus on ritual over relationship

- Elevate rules above grace

- Promote external appearance over internal transformation

- Serve human pride, status, or tradition rather than God

- Use fear and guilt as tools for control

This kind of religion places heavy burdens on people without offering hope. It measures spiritual worth by performance, divides believers through legalism, and distorts God's love into something conditional. It's what Jesus rebuked when He called the Pharisees "whitewashed tombs"—beautiful on the outside but spiritually dead on the inside (Matthew 23:27).

Why the Difference Matters?

The difference between true religion and man-centered religion is the difference between *freedom* and *bondage*, between *authenticity* and *performance*. One draws you closer to God, while the other pushes you into self-reliance or spiritual exhaustion.

Man-centered religion can cause deep wounds. It can make people feel like they're never enough. It can drive people away from church, from community, and even from God. That's why Jesus spoke so forcefully against it—not because He was against religion, but because He was against *religious systems that failed to reflect the heart of God.*

How to Embrace True Religion and Reject the False

Stay Rooted in Scripture: Let God's Word be your standard—not religious tradition, popular opinion, or human teaching. Test everything against the truth of Scripture.

Pursue Relationship Over Routine: Make space in your life to know God personally. Religion without relationship is empty. Relationship without religion often lacks structure. The healthiest faith includes both—but prioritizes the heart behind the habit.

Stay Humble: True religion produces humility. It reminds us that we are all in need of grace, no matter how long we've been following Christ. Avoid the trap of comparing your walk to someone else's.

Serve in Love, Not Obligation: Acts of service and obedience should flow from gratitude, not guilt. If you're doing things for God out of fear or pressure, pause and ask Him to renew your motivation.

Watch for Fruit, Not Just Form: Jesus said we would know people by their fruit (Matthew 7:16). Look for love, joy, peace, patience, kindness, and humility—not just religious activity.

Final Thoughts

Religion, as God designed it, is beautiful. It's a reflection of worship, discipline, and devotion that flows from a life changed by grace. But man-centered religion is a counterfeit. It binds instead of frees, divides instead of unites, and performs instead of transforms. The answer is not to abandon religion altogether—it's to reject the version shaped by human pride and return to the one grounded in God's Word and empowered by His Spirit. Let your faith be real, humble, and rooted in Christ—not in the performance of man, but in the presence of God.

Taking Action

Think | Write | Grow

Based on what you learned in this chapter:

What's something you will stop doing or a habit you will break?

_____

_____

What's something you will start doing or a habit you will create?

_____

_____

What's the potential positive impact of improving in this area?

_____

_____

Chapter Sixteen

Relationship Is Better Than Rituals

Rival 3: Religion

In a world filled with traditions, customs, and sacred routines, it's easy to confuse religious activity with spiritual intimacy. Church attendance, Bible reading, prayers before meals, reciting creeds, or observing holy days can become automatic habits that give the appearance of devotion. But the heart of Christianity was never meant to be built on ritual alone. At its core, the Gospel is not about man-centered rules and routines—it's about *relationship with God*. A real, vibrant, living relationship with the Holy God who created us.

Religious rituals have their place. They can provide structure, remind us of spiritual truths, draw us into moments of reflection, and create an environment for fellowship with other believers. But without a genuine connection to God, rituals become empty motions—checkboxes that check nothing off in Heaven. God is not looking for religious performance; He is seeking our hearts. And nothing compares to knowing Him personally.

Jesus Didn't Die for Man-Centered Religion—He Died for Relationship

When Jesus came to Earth, He didn't blend in with the religious elite. In fact, He reserved His strongest words for those who looked holy on the outside but were spiritually empty inside. In Matthew 23:27, He said, *"Woe to you, teachers of the law and Pharisees, you hypocrites! You are like whitewashed tombs, which look beautiful on the outside but on the inside are full of the bones of the dead."*

The Pharisees were obsessed with rituals. They knew the law, performed the ceremonies, and followed strict rules. But they missed the very heart of God. Meanwhile, tax collectors, sinners, and broken people found life—not by following a formula—but by falling at the feet of Jesus. Religion without relationship is man-centered and spiritually dead. But a relationship with God brings everything to life.

Ritual Without Relationship Invites Distance

Religious practices, on their own, keep God at arm's length. It says, *"I'll give You an hour on Sunday,"* or *"I'll recite these prayers and go through the motions."* It looks good publicly but rarely transforms privately. But a relationship with God changes how you live, how you think, and who you become—because it's based on *intimacy*, not image.

John 15:15 captures this beautifully. Jesus told His disciples, *"I no longer call you servants... Instead, I have called you friends."* Friends don't need rituals to connect—they need honesty, trust, time, and love. That's what God desires with us: not religious appearances, but relational depth.

Rituals Focus on Performance—Relationship Focuses on Presence

Religious rituals can quickly become about *doing*. Did I pray long enough? Did I say the right words? Did I read enough chapters? But a relationship with God isn't about checking off spiritual tasks—it's about being in His presence.

Psalm 16:11 says, *"In Your presence there is fullness of joy."* Not in performance. Not in religious striving. But in presence. God wants you to sit with Him, walk with Him, talk to Him, and listen for His voice. It's not about ritual perfection, but about relational connection.

God Looks at the Heart More Than the Habit

It's possible to do all the "right" things and still be far from God. Jesus said in Matthew 15:8, *"These people honor me with their lips, but their hearts are far from me."* That's the danger of ritual-driven religion—it can mask a disconnected heart.

God cares more about *why* you do something than *what* you do. Are you going to church out of guilt or out of love? Are you praying because you want to know Him or because you feel obligated? The answer reveals your spiritual reality more than the ritual itself.

Relationship Leads to Transformation

Religious rituals may be good for building relationships with fellow Christians, but only a relationship with God leads to lasting transformation. When you truly walk with Jesus—when you surrender your heart, not just your habits—you begin to change from the inside out.

2 Corinthians 5:17 promises, *"If anyone is in Christ, the new creation has come: The old has gone, the new is here!"* Rituals alone can't make you new. Religion alone can't save your soul. But Jesus can. He came to give you life—*not a* to-do *list*.

Rituals Serve a Purpose—But They Shouldn't Be the Goal

It's important to note that rituals themselves aren't bad. Reading the Bible, praying, fasting, and taking communion are all important biblical practices. But they are tools—not trophies. They help *nurture* your relationship with God and with people, but they are not a *substitute* for the relationship that matters most. If rituals lead you into deeper communion with Christ and with fellow believers, they're useful. But if they replace your need for Him, they've become costly distractions.

Final Thoughts

God is not impressed by empty words or religious showmanship. He doesn't want your ritual in and of itself—He wants *you.* Your honest heart. Your messy faith. Your real questions. Your quiet trust. That's what moves His heart. Christianity is not a religion of rituals—it's a relationship built on grace, love, and truth. Don't settle for a lifeless routine when you've been invited into intimate fellowship with the living God. Are you willing to move beyond the ritual and step into the life-changing relationship God created you for?

Taking Action

Think | Write | Grow

Based on what you learned in this chapter:

What's something you will stop doing or a habit you will break?

_____

_____

What's something you will start doing or a habit you will create?

_____

_____

What's the potential positive impact of improving in this area?

_____

_____

Chapter Seventeen

Grace Is Unearned and Undeserved

Rival 3: Religion

I n a world that constantly tells us to earn our worth—to perform, achieve, and prove ourselves—it's easy to carry that same mindset into our relationship with God. We start believing that the more we pray, serve, give, or behave, the more God will love us. We measure our spiritual progress by how well we perform. And when we fail, we feel ashamed, distant, or disqualified.

But grace doesn't operate on human terms. Grace isn't earned through effort or deserved through good behavior. Grace is God's unearned, undeserved, and unrepayable favor toward us—freely given through Jesus Christ.

Grace dismantles every performance-based system we've built. It silences the voice that says, *"You're not doing enough."* It shatters the illusion that God's love depends on our perfection, and it reminds us that our identity in Christ is based not on what we *do*, but on what He *has done*.

Grace Begins Where Our Strength Ends

Ephesians 2:8–9 says it plainly: *"For it is by grace you have been saved, through faith—and this is not from yourselves, it is the gift of God—not by works, so that no one can boast."* Salvation doesn't come from our performance. It comes from God's mercy. No one earns their way into heaven. No amount of rule-keeping or righteous living makes us more lovable to God.

Grace means that Jesus did for us what we could never do for ourselves. He lived a perfect life, died a sacrificial death, and rose again—not because we deserved it, but because we *needed* it. Our best efforts fall short of God's standard of holiness, but His grace bridges the gap.

Performance Mentality is the Enemy of Peace

Many Christians live as if grace saved them, but performance will keep them saved. They begin with grace but quickly fall into striving—trying to win God's approval through religious activity. They feel pressure to be flawless, to never miss a devotion, and to always "feel spiritual."

This performance mentality robs us of joy. It leaves us exhausted, anxious, and fearful of failure. But God doesn't love us more on our best days, and He doesn't love us less on our worst. His love is rooted in His character, not our behavior.

Romans 5:8 reminds us, *"But God demonstrates his own love for us in this: While we were still sinners, Christ died for us."* Grace didn't wait for us to perform—it reached for us while we were broken.

You Can't Work for a Gift

Imagine someone giving you a priceless gift, and instead of receiving it with gratitude, you pull out your wallet and try to pay them back. That's what many Christians do with grace. They try to earn what has already been freely given.

But Romans 11:6 says, *"And if by grace, then it cannot be based on works; if it were, grace would no longer be grace."* Grace that can be earned isn't grace at all—it's a wage. And God is not handing out paychecks. He's offering forgiveness, healing, and eternal life—for free. The right response to grace is *gratitude*, not guilt. *Trust*, not striving.

Grace Doesn't Excuse Sin—It Empowers Change

Some people misunderstand grace as a license to live however they want. But true grace doesn't make us want to sin more—it makes us want to worship more. Grace transforms the heart. It doesn't just save us from punishment—it draws us into a deeper relationship with God.

Titus 2:11–12 says, *"For the grace of God has appeared that offers salvation to all people. It teaches us to say 'No' to ungodliness and worldly passions, and to live self-controlled, upright and godly lives in this present age."*

Grace doesn't lower the standard—it gives us the power through the Holy Spirit to live according to it, not because we have to earn God's love, but because we already have it.

You Are Fully Loved, Right Now

The most freeing truth a Christian can embrace is knowing that you are already fully loved, accepted, and valued in Christ—right now. Not someday when you get it together. Not when your devotional life improves. Not when you overcome every sin. But right now. Grace meets you where you are, not where you think you should be. It covers your past, empowers your present, and secures your future.

Final Thoughts

The Christian life is not about achieving—it's about *abiding*. It's not about earning—it's about *receiving*. Grace is not a reward for good behavior—it's a rescue for the broken. And every day you walk with God is not a performance—it's a relationship grounded in mercy. Don't let a performance mindset keep you from resting in the truth of the Gospel. Grace is unearned. It's undeserved. And it's more than enough. Are you ready to stop striving and start living in the freedom that only grace can provide?

Taking Action

Think | Write | Grow

Based on what you learned in this chapter:

What's something you will stop doing or a habit you will break?

_____

_____

What's something you will start doing or a habit you will create?

_____

_____

What's the potential positive impact of improving in this area?

_____

_____

Chapter Eighteen

Legalism Binds and Grace Liberates

Rival 3: Religion

C hristianity was never meant to be a cage of rules, checklists, and endless striving. Yet, for many, faith has become more about *doing* than *being*, more about appearances than authenticity. This is the trap of legalism—a distorted version of Christianity that says your worth is tied to your performance, that God's love must be earned, and that outward conformity is more important than inner transformation.

Legalism blinds. It narrows your vision. It turns a vibrant relationship with God into a lifeless ritual. But grace—God's unearned, undeserved favor—*liberates*. It opens your eyes to the truth: that you are loved, accepted, and made righteous not because of what you do, but because of what Christ has already done.

Legalism Focuses on Rules—Grace Focuses on Relationship

Legalism says, *"Do more, try harder, earn your place."* It thrives on performance, measuring spiritual worth by how perfectly you follow the rules. It often reduces the Christian life to external behavior, such as how you dress, how often you attend church, how long you pray, or how many verses you memorize. But while these things may look holy, they can become hollow if disconnected from a real relationship with God.

Jesus warned about this in Matthew 23:27: *"Woe to you, teachers of the law and Pharisees, you hypocrites! You are like whitewashed tombs, which look beautiful on the outside but on the inside are full of the bones of the dead."* Legalism cleans the surface but ignores the soul.

Grace, on the other hand, says, *"Come as you are and walk with Me."* It doesn't lower the standard—it changes the source of your righteousness. Grace shifts the focus from trying to impress God and people to trusting in *Jesus*, who already fulfilled the law on our behalf.

Legalism Leads to Pride or Despair—Grace Leads to Peace

Legalism is a cruel taskmaster. If you think you're doing well, it breeds *pride*—you look down on others, believing you're spiritually superior. If you fail (and you will), it leads to *despair*—you feel like you've disappointed God and have to earn your way back. This constant seesaw of pride and shame creates anxiety, burnout, and spiritual insecurity. You never feel good enough, clean enough, or faithful enough. But grace silences that noise. Romans 5:1 says, *"Therefore, since we have been justified through faith, we have peace with God through our Lord Jesus Christ."* That peace comes not from perfection, but from *position*—being securely placed in Christ.

Legalism Blinds Us to Our Need for Grace

One of the most dangerous effects of legalism is that it makes us believe we don't need grace—or that we've outgrown it. Like the Pharisee in Luke 18, legalistic believers may pray, *"Thank you, God, that I'm not like other people."* They mistake discipline for holiness, rule-following for righteousness. But the Bible is clear: *"All have sinned and fall short of the glory of God"* (Romans 3:23). Grace is not a backup plan for sinners—it's the foundation of salvation. Without it, we are spiritually blind, regardless of how clean our record looks. Grace opens our eyes to our true condition, not to condemn us, but to *redeem* us.

Grace Empowers What Legalism Can't

Legalism demands change but offers no power to produce it. It says, *"Stop sinning,"* but doesn't tell you how. It burdens people with guilt but doesn't give them strength. Grace does the opposite. Titus 2:11–12 says, *"For the grace of God has* appeared, *that offers salvation to all people. It teaches us to say 'No' to ungodliness... and to live self-controlled, upright, and godly lives."* Grace doesn't just forgive—it *empowers*. It changes your heart from the inside out, aligning your desires with God's, not out of fear, but out of love. It gives you a reason to obey that legalism never could—*gratitude*.

Jesus Came to Set Us Free from Legalism

When Jesus walked the earth, His goal was not to start another religion. He did, however, desire to set us free from the burden of man-centered, performance-based religions. In Matthew 11:28–30, He said, *"Come to me, all you who are weary and burdened, and I will give you rest... For my yoke is easy and my burden is light."* That "weary and burdened" life? That's legalism. Jesus was offering something better—*rest for your soul.* Not spiritual laziness, but spiritual liberty. Not a life without obedience, but a life where obedience flows from love, not fear.

Final Thoughts

Legalism may look holy, but it lacks life. It blinds us with rules, drowns us in guilt, and hides us from the freedom Christ died to give. Grace, on the other hand, liberates us. It gives us clarity, confidence, and communion with God. If you're tired of performing, striving, or feeling like you're never enough, it's time to lay down the burden of legalism and embrace the gift of grace. You don't have to earn what's already been given. You just have to receive it. Are you ready to stop striving and start living in the freedom that grace provides?

Taking Action

Think | Write | Grow

Based on what you learned in this chapter:

What's something you will stop doing or a habit you will break?

_____

_____

What's something you will start doing or a habit you will create?

_____

_____

What's the potential positive impact of improving in this area?

_____

_____

Chapter Nineteen

The Ultimate Honor Belongs to God

Rival 3: Religion

O ne of the greatest threats to authentic faith isn't always found in the world outside the Church—it often arises within it. While religion can be a vehicle for teaching God's truth and fostering spiritual growth, it also has a dangerous potential—it can elevate human leaders above their rightful place, putting them on pedestals meant only for God. When this happens, faith becomes distorted, loyalty becomes misdirected, and the authority of man begins to replace the authority of God.

This subtle but dangerous shift often starts with good intentions. A gifted pastor, teacher, or spiritual leader inspires people, leads with passion, and teaches biblical truth. But over time, admiration becomes idolization. Respect becomes reverence. Trust becomes dependency. And without realizing it, a leader's voice starts to carry more weight than Scripture itself.

The Problem of Pedestals

God never intended for any human leader to become the centerpiece of faith. Even the greatest figures in Scripture—Moses, David, Paul—were deeply flawed and were never meant to be worshiped. But religion, when driven by culture instead of conviction, has a tendency to exalt charisma over character and visibility over humility.

This culture of celebrity Christianity is increasingly common. Leaders gain massive followings, build personal brands, and are treated as untouchable. Their opinions become gospel. Their failures are overlooked. Their word is rarely challenged. But the danger is clear: the higher we lift a person, the further they have to fall—and the more damage it causes when they do. When leaders are placed on pedestals, two things can happen—they can become isolated and prideful, and their followers can become spiritually dependent. Neither scenario is healthy, and both are contrary to how God designed the Church to function.

When Human Authority Replaces God's Voice

One of the clearest signs that religion has gone off course is when people begin to follow a leader more than they follow God. It can look spiritual on the surface—quoting pastors more than Scripture, attending events rather than pursuing personal intimacy with God, or prioritizing denominational loyalty over biblical truth.

But Jesus never said, "Follow my servants." He said, *"Follow Me."* In Matthew 23:9–10, He warned the religious crowd, *"Do not call anyone on earth 'father,' for you have one Father, and he is in heaven. Nor are you to be called instructors, for you have one Instructor, the Messiah."*

The Church is called to be a body, not a hierarchy of human idols. While leaders can play important roles, they are *shepherds*, not saviors; *messengers*, not masters. Their authority must always be submitted to the authority of Christ.

The Spiritual Fallout of Leader Worship

When leaders are idolized, the fallout is far-reaching. First, it creates disillusionment. If a leader fails morally, spiritually, or personally (and many eventually do), those who placed their hope in that leader often walk away—not just from the church, but from God Himself. They confuse a flawed human with a flawless Savior.

Second, it stunts spiritual maturity. When people rely solely on a leader's guidance, they often neglect their personal relationship with God. They stop studying Scripture for themselves, stop listening to the Holy Spirit, and stop growing in spiritual discernment.

Lastly, it invites pride and corruption in the leader. Proverbs 16:18 warns, *"Pride goes before destruction, a haughty spirit before a fall."* When leaders begin to believe their own hype, they lose the humility required to lead others by setting a Godly example.

Biblical Leadership: A Model of Humility and Service

Jesus modeled a radically different kind of leadership—one grounded in servanthood and submission to the Father. In John 13, He washed His disciples' feet, saying, *"I have set you an example that you should do as I have done for you."* True Christian leadership never demands to be served—it *serves*.

Paul, too, constantly deflected glory. In 1 Corinthians 3:5–7, he writes, *"What, after all, is Apollos? And what is Paul? Only servants... So neither the one who plants nor the one who waters is anything, but only God, who makes things grow."* That's the posture every leader should carry—and the posture every believer should expect.

Keep Your Eyes on Christ

If your faith is rooted in a person, it will eventually be shaken. But if your faith is rooted in Christ, it will stand through every storm, scandal, or disappointment. Hebrews 12:2 tells us to *"fix our eyes on Jesus, the author and perfecter of our faith."* Not on pastors. Not on influencers. On *Jesus*. Respect your leaders, honor their role, but never elevate them to a place only God deserves. Leaders can inspire you—but only Jesus can save you.

Final Thoughts

Religion has the power to guide us to God—but it also has the power to distract us from Him if we place people above His Word. No man or woman, no matter how gifted, should sit on the throne of your heart. Let leaders point you *to* God—not replace Him. Let grace keep you humble. Let truth keep you grounded. And let Christ alone remain the center of your worship and trust. Are you following a person—or following the Savior?

Taking Action

Think | Write | Grow

Based on what you learned in this chapter:

What's something you will stop doing or a habit you will break?

_____

_____

What's something you will start doing or a habit you will create?

_____

_____

What's the potential positive impact of improving in this area?

_____

_____

Chapter Twenty

Faith Opposes Self-Righteousness

Rival 3: Religion

R eligion, when rightly practiced, can be a beautiful expression of faith. It can provide structure, community, and tools that help us grow in our relationship with God. But without humility, self-awareness, and a heart anchored in grace, religion can quietly become a breeding ground for self-righteousness—a subtle yet dangerous attitude that places confidence in our own moral performance rather than in God's mercy.

Self-righteousness is deceptive. It dresses itself in piety, discipline, and spiritual lingo, but underneath, it is often rooted in pride. It doesn't lead us closer to God—it leads us to a distorted view of ourselves and others. If we are not careful, the very religion meant to draw us to grace can become a system that props up our egos.

What Is Self-Righteousness?

Self-righteousness is the belief that our worth, righteousness, or closeness to God is based on *our own behavior, knowledge, or spiritual practices.* It often looks like a strong religious life—praying regularly, attending church, reading the Bible—but with a heart that subtly believes, *"I'm better than others because I do these things."*

Jesus directly confronted this attitude in Luke 18:9–14, where He told the parable of the Pharisee and the tax collector. The Pharisee proudly listed his spiritual credentials: *"I fast twice a week and give a tenth of all I get."* Meanwhile, the tax collector simply cried out, *"God, have mercy on me, a sinner."* Jesus said it was the humble man—not the proud one—who went home justified before God.

How Religion Can Feed Self-Righteousness

Religion becomes dangerous when it turns inward—when the focus shifts from relationship with God to self-performance. Here are a few ways religion can unintentionally feed a self-righteous mindset:

1. Comparison: Measuring our spirituality by comparing ourselves to others—"At least I'm not like *them*."

2. Checklist Faith: Treating spiritual disciplines like tasks that prove our worth instead of tools that draw us closer to God.

3. Judgmental: Assuming moral superiority and a quickness to condemn others whose struggles are different than ours.

4. Pride in Knowledge: Believing that knowing Scripture or theology makes us more valuable in God's eyes or better than others.

5. External Focus: Emphasizing appearances, rituals, and religious behavior while ignoring the condition of the heart.

In all these cases, the danger is not in the practice itself—but in the posture of the heart. When the focus of religion becomes *us*, we've lost the essence of true and innocent faith.

Why Is Self-Righteousness Dangerous?

Self-righteousness blinds us to our own need for grace. It creates spiritual pride, which not only separates us from others but distances us from God. James 4:6 warns, *"God opposes the proud but shows favor to the humble."* When we become self-righteous, we are no longer relying on Christ—we are relying on ourselves. It also damages our witness. A self-righteous Christian often comes across as harsh, hypocritical, and unapproachable. Instead of drawing people to Christ, they push people away by portraying a faith that feels more like moral elitism than mercy.

How to Guard Against Self-Righteousness

1. Stay Rooted in Grace
   Never forget that everything you are in Christ is because of what *He* has done—not what you've done. Ephesians 2:8–9 reminds us, *"For*

it is by grace you have been saved, through faith... not by works, so that no one can boast." The more you reflect on God's grace, the less room pride will have to grow.

2. Practice Heart Examination
Regularly ask God to search your heart. Psalm 139:23–24 says, *"Search me, God, and know my heart... see if there is any offensive way in me."* Invite the Holy Spirit to reveal any attitudes of superiority, comparison, or pride that may have taken root.

3. Pursue Humility, Not Applause
Jesus said in Matthew 6:1, *"Be careful not to practice your righteousness in front of others to be seen by them."* Do good in secret. Serve without needing credit. Pray without showcasing it. Humility is the antidote to self-righteousness.

4. Remember Your Own Brokenness
Never lose sight of what God saved you from. Romans 3:23 declares, *"For all have sinned and fall short of the glory of God."* When you remember your own need for grace, it becomes easier to extend it to others.

5. Stay Relational, Not Just Religious
Faith is not about checking boxes—it's about walking with God. Don't just go through the motions of religion. Engage with your heart. Speak with God daily. Let Scripture transform you, not just inform you.

Final Thoughts

Religion without humility can quickly become self-worship dressed in spiritual clothing. When we start to believe that our righteousness comes from our efforts, we've traded the Gospel for a glorified performance. But there is a better way. A life rooted in grace, marked by humility, and fueled by love is far more powerful than one built on self-effort. Jesus didn't call us to earn our way to God—He called us to admit our need and follow Him. Are you building your faith through grace—or on your own performance? Choose the path that leads to grace.

Taking Action

Think | Write | Grow

Based on what you learned in this chapter:

What's something you will stop doing or a habit you will break?

_____

_____

What's something you will start doing or a habit you will create?

_____

_____

What's the potential positive impact of improving in this area?

_____

_____

Chapter Twenty-One

God Has Not Given Us a Spirit of Fear

Rival 3: Religion

F ear can be a powerful motivator—but when used wrongly, it becomes a spiritual weapon of control. Sadly, many Christians, while seeking to grow in faith, find themselves bound not by sin, but by *religious fear*. They are afraid of failure, afraid of judgment, afraid of losing God's love, or of being cast out of their community for not measuring up. But this kind of fear is not from God.

2 Timothy 1:7 makes it clear: *"For God has not given us a spirit of fear, but of power, and of love, and of a sound mind."* God's voice does not manipulate or threaten—He leads with truth and love. When religion begins to control Christians through fear, it distorts the Gospel and robs believers of the freedom Jesus died to give.

So, how can we recognize when fear-based religion has crept in, and how do we guard against it?

1. Understand the Difference Between Conviction and Condemnation

One of the most important distinctions in the Christian life is between conviction (from the Holy Spirit) and condemnation (from the enemy—or fear-based teaching). Conviction gently leads you to repentance. It says, *"You've sinned, but God is ready to forgive. Come back."* Condemnation, on the other hand, says, *"You're hopeless. You've failed. God is done with you."*

If your faith walk is dominated by shame, dread, or fear of being cast aside, that's not the voice of your Shepherd. Romans 8:1 affirms this truth: *"There-fore, there is now no condemnation for those who are in Christ Jesus."* Watch out for any message or teaching that heaps guilt without pointing to grace.

2. Beware of Leadership That Uses Fear to Control

In healthy Christian leadership, shepherds guide their people toward a deeper relationship with Jesus, not stricter adherence to man-centered rules. But in some religious environments, fear becomes a tool to maintain control. Leaders may imply that questioning their authority is equivalent to questioning God. Or, they might threaten divine punishment for stepping outside the group's boundaries.

This is spiritual manipulation, and it contradicts the servant-hearted leadership Jesus modeled. In Matthew 20:25–26, He said, *"The rulers of the Gentiles lord it over them... Not so with you. Instead, whoever wants to become great among you must be your servant."* If your spiritual leaders are using fear instead of love, or intimidation instead of instruction, it's a red flag.

3. Legalism Feeds on Fear

Legalism—the belief that your worth or salvation is dependent on your performance—is one of the most common roots of fear-based religion. It teaches that if you don't follow every rule exactly, you're in danger of losing God's favor. It reduces faith to formulas and burdens people with guilt for not doing enough.

But Ephesians 2:8–9 reminds us: *"For it is by grace you have been saved, through faith—and this is not from yourselves, it is the gift of God—not by works, so that no one can boast."* God's love is not fragile. It does not disappear when you fail. His grace doesn't break under pressure—it *covers* you in mercy.

4. Watch for a Culture of Fear Instead of Freedom

In a fear-based religious culture, you might find people who are always anxious, perfectionistic, or critical. They're afraid of messing up, saying the wrong thing, or expressing doubt. There's little room for honest struggle, questions, or failure. People stay silent out of fear of being judged or excluded. This is not the environment Jesus came to create. 2 Corinthians 3:17 tells us, *"Where the Spirit of the Lord is, there is freedom."* A healthy church or Christian community should be a place of grace, not fear, and of growth, not guilt.

5. Test the Message by the Fruit It Produces

Jesus said in Matthew 7:16, *"You will recognize them by their fruits."* If a message or religious culture consistently produces anxiety, shame, pride, judgment, or division, it is not bearing the fruit of the Spirit. The fruit of the Spirit is love, joy, peace, patience, kindness, goodness, faithfulness, gentleness, and self-control (Galatians 5:22–23). These fruits grow in environments rooted in *grace and truth*, not in fear and control.

6. Anchor Your Identity in Christ, Not in Performance

The antidote to fear-based religion is to root your identity in the finished work of Jesus. You are not defined by how many rules you follow, how often you serve, or how perfect your behavior is. You are defined by the righteousness of Christ. Colossians 2:6–7 encourages us: *"So then, just as you received Christ Jesus as Lord, continue to live your lives in him, rooted and built up in him."* Stay rooted in *Him*, not in human systems or performance checklists.

Final Thoughts

God never intended for Christianity to be driven by fear. The Gospel is an invitation to freedom, not a sentence of slavery. Jesus didn't come to build another man-centered religion rooted in control. Instead, He came to set the captives free (Luke 4:18). Be watchful of teachings that intimidate rather than inspire. Be cautious of leaders who manipulate rather than mentor. And always come back to the truth: God has not given you a spirit of fear, but of power, love, and a sound mind. Are you following the voice of fear—or the voice of your loving Father? One leads to bondage. The other to freedom. Choose God's freedom.

Taking Action

Think | Write | Grow

Based on what you learned in this chapter:

What's something you will stop doing or a habit you will break?

_____

_____

What's something you will start doing or a habit you will create?

_____

_____

What's the potential positive impact of improving in this area?

_____

_____

RIVAL 4

--- ◆ ---

IGNORANCE

"Learn God's Word"

Chapter Twenty-Two

Ignorance Can Become Knowledge

Rival 4: Ignorance

T he Bible is, by all accounts, the best-selling book of all time. It has been translated into over 3,000 languages, printed in the billions, and distributed in every corner of the world. It's been read by kings and prisoners, quoted by presidents and poets, and treasured by millions as the Word of God. Yet, despite its reach and reverence, a surprising and sobering truth remains: many people are still deeply ignorant of what the Bible actually says.

Owning a Bible is not the same as *knowing* it. Quoting a verse is not the same as *understanding* it. And referencing Scripture does not mean someone is *living* by it. In an age where information is more accessible than ever, biblical literacy is, ironically, on the decline. The very book that claims to contain the words of life is often unread, misunderstood, or misused—even by those who call themselves Christians.

A Global Bestseller, a Personal Stranger

It's estimated that over 5 billion copies of the Bible have been printed since its origin. It outsells every major book annually and is consistently at the top of every sales chart, though often excluded due to its overwhelming dominance. From Gutenberg's printing press in the 15th century to Bible apps in the 21st, the Bible continues to spread. And yet, the question remains: Why is the world's most printed and purchased book so often ignored in practice?

Part of the problem lies in assumptions. Many people grow up with the Bible in their home, at their church, or in their cultural background, so they assume they already know what it says. Others have heard it misquoted or misrepresented and assume they know enough to dismiss it. Still others are intimidated by its length, language, or complexity, so they leave it untouched.

The Danger of Biblical Ignorance

Not knowing the Bible isn't just a missed opportunity for spiritual growth—it's a dangerous vacuum. When people are unfamiliar with Scripture, they become vulnerable to false teaching, cultural confusion, and personal compromise.

Jesus warned in Matthew 22:29, *"You are in error because you do not know the Scriptures or the power of God."* This warning still applies today. People form opinions about God, morality, purpose, and eternity based not on truth but on emotion, tradition, or popular opinion. Without the anchor of Scripture, we are easily swayed by whatever seems appealing in the moment.

Even within the Church, biblical illiteracy has become a growing concern. Studies show that many churchgoers cannot name the Ten Commandments, recall basic Bible stories, or explain the Gospel clearly. The Bible is referenced in sermons, but not always read in daily life. It's quoted in songs but often missing from conversations.

A Book Meant to Be Opened, Not Just Owned

The Bible isn't just a historical artifact or a religious symbol—it's a living and active Word (Hebrews 4:12). It wasn't meant to sit on a shelf, but to shape our hearts. It wasn't written to collect dust, but to ignite transformation.

Psalm 119:105 says, *"Your word is a lamp for my feet, a light on my path."* But how can it guide us if we don't open it? How can we say we follow Jesus if we don't read the book that reveals who He is?

The Bible is more than a source of moral principles. It's the story of redemption. From Genesis to Revelation, it reveals God's character, humanity's need, and Christ's victory. It speaks to every part of life—family, leadership, justice, suffering, and eternity.

Why We Must Rediscover the Bible

We are living in a time when truth is often relative, feelings trump facts, and opinions are mistaken for authority. In such a climate, we need the clarity and foundation the Bible provides more than ever.

If you're a believer, the Bible is not optional—it's essential. 2 Timothy 3:16-17 reminds us that *"All Scripture is God-breathed and is useful for teaching, rebuking, correcting, and training in righteousness, so that the servant of God may be thoroughly equipped for every good work."*

If you're not a Christian, the Bible still offers unmatched wisdom, timeless truths, and a compelling account of God's pursuit of humanity. But to understand its message, you have to read it with an open heart and a seeking mind.

Final Thoughts

It's a tragedy to own the most powerful book ever written—and never open it. The Bible is the best-selling book of all time, but for many, it remains the least-read. We don't suffer from a lack of access—we suffer from a lack of engagement. It's time to dust it off. To dig in. To move beyond casual familiarity and into genuine understanding. Because the Bible doesn't just inform—it transforms. Don't just own a Bible. Let it own your heart. Read it. Know it. Live it.

Taking Action

Think | Write | Grow

Based on what you learned in this chapter:

What's something you will stop doing or a habit you will break?

_____

_____

What's something you will start doing or a habit you will create?

_____

_____

What's the potential positive impact of improving in this area?

_____

_____

Chapter Twenty-Three

Wisdom Begins With Knowledge of God

Rival 4: Ignorance

I n an age overflowing with information, knowledge is everywhere. From scientific breakthroughs to philosophical debates, from leadership strategies to self-help mantras, the modern world prides itself on being more educated and connected than ever before. And yet, with all this knowledge, many still lack *wisdom*. People know how to build cities, lead corporations, and program machines, but they often struggle to build strong character, lead their homes, find their sense of purpose, or navigate life's deepest questions.

Why? Because true wisdom doesn't start with knowledge of the world—it begins with the knowledge of God.

The Foundation of Wisdom: Knowing God

The Bible is clear about where wisdom originates. Proverbs 9:10 declares, *"The fear of the Lord is the beginning of wisdom, and knowledge of the Holy One is understanding."* This isn't about being afraid of God in a cowering sense; it's about having deep reverence, awe, and submission to Him. To fear the Lord means to recognize His holiness, authority, and sovereignty—and to align your life accordingly.

You cannot separate wisdom from God because God *is* the source of all wisdom. He is the Creator of the universe, the Author of life, the One who designed human purpose and destiny. To live wisely, then, is to live in harmony with His truth, His ways, and His character.

The Word of God: Our Map to Wisdom

If the knowledge of God is the beginning of wisdom, then the Word of God is the pathway to it. The Bible is not just a religious book filled with ancient history and moral stories—it is God's revealed truth, given to guide us, teach us, and shape our understanding of life.

Psalm 119:130 says, *"The unfolding of your words gives light; it gives understanding to the simple."* In other words, even those who feel lost, confused, or uneducated can walk in wisdom—if they turn to the light of Scripture.

God's Word addresses every area of life: family, relationships, finances, leadership, morality, suffering, purpose, and eternity. It not only shows us what to do, but it teaches us *why* it matters and *how* to live it out. It gives us both principles and perspective, something that worldly knowledge often fails to do.

The Difference Between Worldly Knowledge and Godly Wisdom

Worldly knowledge teaches you how to climb the ladder of success. Godly wisdom teaches you *which ladder is worth climbing*? Worldly knowledge can tell you how to build a marriage, but godly wisdom tells you how to love sacrificially and forgive endlessly. Worldly knowledge can help you get more, do more, and become more. But godly wisdom reminds you that *who* you are becoming is more important than what you are achieving.

1 Corinthians 3:19 says, *"For the wisdom of this world is foolishness in God's sight."* This is not a condemnation of science, learning, or progress—it's a warning not to elevate human intellect above divine truth. Any wisdom that denies the authority of God and His Word is ultimately hollow and unstable.

Wisdom Is More Than Intelligence—It's Obedience

Biblical wisdom is not just about knowing the right answers—it's about walking in the right direction. Jesus said in Matthew 7:24, *"Therefore everyone who hears these words of mine and puts them into practice is like a wise man who built his house on the rock."* Wisdom isn't found in hearing alone, but in *doing*—in applying God's Word to your daily life.

Many people have heard Scripture, read devotionals, or attended church for years, but their lives remain unchanged because they've never acted on what they've heard. Wisdom isn't stored in the mind—it's revealed through the choices we make and the fruit we bear.

Why We Desperately Need God's Wisdom Today

We live in a world that is morally confused, emotionally overwhelmed, and spiritually numb. Technology has advanced, but discernment has declined. We have louder opinions, but less truth. More information, yet fewer answers. In times like these, we don't just need more data—we need *divine direction.*

James 1:5 offers this promise: *"If any of you lacks wisdom, you should ask God, who gives generously to all without finding fault, and it will be given to you."* God isn't hiding wisdom from us—He's offering it to those who seek Him sincerely.

Final Thoughts

All wisdom begins—not with degrees, status, or life experience—but with a deep, reverent knowledge of God and His Word. Without that foundation, our knowledge is unanchored, and our lives become vulnerable to deception, confusion, and collapse. But when we build our lives on the rock of God's truth, we gain more than intelligence—we gain clarity, discernment, peace, and purpose. We are equipped to make decisions that honor God, bless others, and lead to lasting fruit. The wisest decision you can make is to seek the One who created wisdom itself. Let God be your teacher, His Word your guide, and His truth your foundation.

Taking Action

Think | Write | Grow

Based on what you learned in this chapter:

What's something you will stop doing or a habit you will break?

_____

_____

What's something you will start doing or a habit you will create?

_____

_____

What's the potential positive impact of improving in this area?

_____

_____

Chapter Twenty-Four

God's Word Is the Standard of Truth

Rival 4: Ignorance

I n a world of shifting values, competing opinions, and ever-changing cultural norms, many people struggle to find something solid to stand on. Truth, once viewed as objective and absolute, is increasingly treated as relative—"your truth" vs. "my truth." But for Christians, there is one unshakable answer to this confusion: God's Word is the ultimate standard for truth.

The Bible is not just a book of moral stories or spiritual inspiration. It is the very revelation of God's mind and heart to humanity. It defines what is true, exposes what is false, and guides how we should live, believe, and worship. For Christians who desire to walk in righteousness, Scripture is not optional—it is foundational.

1. Truth Is Not a Concept—It's a Person

Jesus made a bold statement in John 14:6: *"I am the way and the truth and the life. No one comes to the Father except through me."* Truth is not just information—it is a person. Jesus embodies truth perfectly because He is the Word made flesh (John 1:14). To know Christ is to know truth. And to know Christ more deeply is to know His Word more faithfully.

God's Word is not disconnected from God Himself. When we read the Bible, we're not just engaging with religious text—we are encountering the living voice of God. That's why 2 Timothy 3:16–17 says, *"All Scripture is God-breathed and is useful for teaching, rebuking,* correcting, *and training in righteousness."* The Bible doesn't just contain truth—it is truth.

2. God's Word Is Unchanging in a Changing World

The world constantly changes its moral compass based on public opinion, political trends, or emotional appeals. But the Word of God remains unchanged. Isaiah 40:8 reminds us, *"The grass withers, the flower fades, but the word of our God will stand forever."*

While culture redefines truth, God has already defined it—and He doesn't update it to suit modern tastes. Psalm 119:160 declares, *"The sum of your word is truth, and every one of your righteous rules endures forever."* What was sin in God's eyes 2,000 years ago is still sin today. What was righteous then is still righteous now.

This unchanging standard is what gives Christians stability. When emotions fluctuate and society shifts, God's Word remains our compass—pointing us to what is right, holy, and pleasing in His sight.

3. The Bible Exposes Lies and Reveals What Is Right

In a world full of deception, half-truths, and spiritual counterfeits, we need a tool that exposes lies—and that's exactly what God's Word does. Hebrews 4:12 says, *"For the word of God is alive and active. Sharper than any double-edged sword... it judges the thoughts and attitudes of the heart."*

False teachers, twisted theology, and cultural ideologies may sound convincing, but if they contradict Scripture, they are not true. God's Word is our filter. It helps us discern between right and wrong, truth and error, conviction and manipulation.

That's why Christians are urged in 1 Thessalonians 5:21 to *"test everything; hold fast what is good."* But the only way to test what is good is by measuring it against the Bible—God's unchanging standard of truth.

4. Scripture Guides Every Area of Life

God's Word doesn't just speak to spiritual matters—it offers wisdom for every aspect of life. It teaches us how to relate to others, how to handle conflict, how to manage finances, how to lead with integrity, and how to find peace in suffering.

Psalm 119:105 says, *"Your word is a lamp to my feet and a light to my path."* God's Word is not a distant set of rules—it is a living guide for everyday life. And when we submit to its authority, we find clarity, peace, and purpose.

God's truth is not meant to oppress—it is meant to liberate. Jesus said in John 8:31–32, *"If you continue in my word, you are truly my disciples. Then you will know the truth, and the truth will set you free."*

5. God's Word Requires Response and Obedience

It's not enough to agree that the Bible is true—we must submit to it. James 1:22 warns, *"Do not merely listen to the word, and so deceive yourselves. Do what it says."* Truth isn't just something to be known—it's something to be lived.

If we say we love God but ignore His Word, we deceive ourselves. True discipleship involves aligning our lives, decisions, and beliefs with what Scripture teaches—even when it's uncomfortable or countercultural.

Final Thoughts

In a world full of noise and confusion, God's Word stands as the ultimate authority for Christians. It is our source of truth, our guardrail in temptation, our light in darkness, and our weapon against deception. Every opinion, every idea, every spiritual claim must be tested against Scripture. Because if it contradicts God's Word, it's not true—no matter how persuasive it sounds. The Bible is not just a book—it is the voice of God. And for every Christian, it must be the standard we live by, the truth we stand on, and the foundation we never abandon.

Taking Action

Think | Write | Grow

Based on what you learned in this chapter:

What's something you will stop doing or a habit you will break?

_____

_____

What's something you will start doing or a habit you will create?

_____

_____

What's the potential positive impact of improving in this area?

_____

_____

Chapter Twenty-Five

If It's From God, You Can't Overthrow It

Rival 4: Ignorance

I n an age where information is everywhere and spiritual voices flood social media, podcasts, pulpits, and books, it's never been easier to be influenced—and misled. Not every teaching that sounds spiritual is rooted in truth. Not every person who claims to speak for God is delivering His message. The Bible warns repeatedly that false teachers will come, and they won't always be easy to spot. That's why knowing the Bible is essential for every Christian. It is our anchor, our measuring stick, and our defense.

2 Timothy 4:3–4 warns, *"For the time will come when people will not put up with sound doctrine. Instead, to suit their own desires, they will gather around them a great number of teachers to say what their itching ears want to hear."* We are living in those times. Many are drawn not to truth, but to comfort. Not to conviction, but to confirmation. The result? Countless people are being deceived by distorted gospels, watered-down truth, and charismatic leaders who twist Scripture for gain. The solution? Know the Word. Live the Word. Test everything by the Word.

Why Knowing the Bible Matters?

God's Word is not just for pastors, scholars, or theologians—it's for *every believer*. When you know Scripture, you're less likely to be swayed by emotion, fooled by charisma, or caught off guard by spiritual half-truths. Jesus Himself used Scripture to combat the lies of Satan in the wilderness (Matthew 4), and He instructed His followers to remain in His Word to truly be His disciples (John 8:31-32).

Here's why Scripture is so powerful against false teaching:

- It reveals the character and nature of God, so you can recognize when someone is misrepresenting Him.

- It gives you discernment, helping you identify when something sounds good but contradicts biblical truth.

- It roots you in truth, so you can stand firm even when culture, emotions, or public opinion shifts.

3 Practical Steps to Protect Yourself from False Teaching

1. Be Rooted in the Word Daily

You can't recognize a counterfeit if you've never studied the original. One of the most effective ways to detect false doctrine is to be *consistently immersed in truth*. That means developing the habit of reading the Bible—not just occasionally or when you're in crisis, but *daily*. It doesn't require hours of study—as little as 10 minutes a day of reading and reflecting can strengthen your discernment.

Psalm 119:11 says, *"I have hidden your word in my heart that I might not sin against you."* The more Scripture you know, the more equipped you are to detect error—because you'll feel the check in your spirit when something doesn't align with God's Word.

Tip: Use a Bible reading plan, study one book at a time, or use a trusted commentary to help you dig deeper. Don't just read—*study* and *apply*.

2. Test Every Teaching Against Scripture

No matter how famous a preacher is, how passionate a speaker sounds, or how viral a post becomes—always test it against the Bible. Acts 17:11 praises the Bereans because they *"examined the Scriptures every day to see if what Paul said was true."* If even Paul's teachings were scrutinized, how much more should we examine what we hear today?

If a teaching contradicts Scripture—even subtly—it's not from God. Some common red flags of false teaching include:

- Dismissing or redefining sin

- Promising blessings without obedience

- Elevating personal revelation above Scripture

- Focusing on self over Christ

- Downplaying the cross, repentance, or the Lordship of Jesus

When in doubt, go to the Word—and ask the Holy Spirit to guide you in truth (John 16:13).

3. Stay Connected to a Healthy, Bible-Teaching Church

God didn't design us to walk alone. The Church is meant to be a place of truth, accountability, and spiritual growth. Being part of a biblically sound community helps you stay grounded. You can ask questions, seek counsel, and receive correction when needed.

Ephesians 4:14–15 says, *"Then we will no longer be infants, tossed back and forth by the waves, and blown here and there by every wind of teaching... Instead, speaking the truth in love, we will grow to become in every respect the mature body of him who is the head, that is, Christ."*

When you're planted in a church that prioritizes the Word, you're far less likely to be swayed by false doctrines or spiritual fads.

Final Thoughts

False teachings are not just "alternative views"—they are dangerous distortions that lead people away from the truth, away from Christ, and into spiritual confusion. The only way to recognize and resist them is to know God's Word deeply and personally. Don't settle for secondhand faith or borrowed knowledge. Open your Bible. Learn it for yourself. Test everything you hear. And stand firm on the truth that never changes. In a world full of deception, the Word of God is your greatest defense. Know it, live it, and you will not be shaken.

Taking Action

Think | Write | Grow

Based on what you learned in this chapter:

What's something you will stop doing or a habit you will break?

_____

_____

What's something you will start doing or a habit you will create?

_____

_____

What's the potential positive impact of improving in this area?

_____

_____

Chapter Twenty-Six

God's Laws Reveal His Character

Rival 4: Ignorance

T he Bible is more than a religious book—it is the living revelation of who God is. From Genesis to Revelation, it tells the story of God's nature, His relationship with humanity, His standards, and His plan of redemption through Jesus Christ. Among the most foundational passages in Scripture are the Ten Commandments, given by God to Moses on Mount Sinai. These commandments are not just rules for behavior—they are a profound reflection of God's character.

When we understand the Ten Commandments within the larger context of Scripture, we discover that they reveal who God is, what He values, and how He desires His people to live in relationship with Him and with one another. Let's explore what the Bible—and especially the Ten Commandments—teach us about the character of God.

1. God is Holy and Worthy of Exclusive Worship

The very first commandment—*"You shall have no other gods before Me"* (Exodus 20:3)—immediately establishes God's uniqueness and holiness. He is not one god among many; He is the only true God, eternal, sovereign, and worthy of total devotion. This commandment reflects God's righteous jealousy (Exodus 34:14), not in a petty or insecure way, but in His unwavering commitment to truth, purity, and relationship with His people.

God's holiness is a major theme throughout the Bible. Isaiah 6:3 says, *"Holy, holy, holy is the Lord Almighty."* He is set apart from all creation, perfect in nature, and entirely without sin. The first commandment reminds us that we are not to chase false gods, idols, or self-made beliefs—we are to fear, love, and serve the one and only holy God.

2. God is Truthful and Desires Honesty

The ninth commandment—*"You shall not bear false witness"*—shows us that God values truth. The Bible tells us that *"It is impossible for God to lie"* (Hebrews 6:18). Everything He says is pure, reliable, and consistent with His nature. God is the source of all truth, and He calls His people to reflect His integrity in their speech and actions.

Similarly, John 14:6 records Jesus saying, *"I am the way, the truth, and the life."* Truth is not just something God speaks—it's who He is. When we live truthfully, we reflect the very nature of our Creator.

3. God is Just and Values Life

The command, *"You shall not murder"* (Exodus 20:13), teaches us about God's value for human life. According to Genesis 1:27, every human being is made in the image of God. That divine imprint gives life immeasurable value. God is a God of justice, and He will not overlook violence, cruelty, or oppression.

Throughout the Bible, God reveals His concern for the weak, the innocent, and the vulnerable. The command to preserve life reflects God's heart for compassion, justice, and the protection of His creation.

4. God is Faithful and Desires Faithfulness

The commandment against adultery—*"You shall not commit adultery"*—reflects God's faithfulness. God never breaks His promises, never abandons His people, and never acts unfaithfully. In fact, the covenant between God and Israel is often compared to a marriage. In the New Testament, the Church is called the "Bride of Christ."

God's character is one of unwavering loyalty, and He calls us to mirror that in our relationships. Faithfulness in marriage and purity in heart reflect a deeper spiritual truth about God's commitment to His people.

5. God is Generous and Just

"You shall not steal" is a command that reflects God's respect for ownership and His desire for justice. God is a provider, and He calls us to trust in His provision rather than take what is not ours. God blesses generously, but He also values stewardship and fairness.

Psalm 145:16 says, *"You open your hand and satisfy the desires of every living thing."* God is not stingy—He is openhanded. And He wants His people to reflect His justice, generosity, and respect for others.

6. God is Relational and Desires Worship from the Heart

The first four commandments deal with humanity's relationship with God. They reveal that God is not distant—He is relational. He desires worship that is sincere, reverent, and personal. He commands us to *"Remember the Sabbath day"* not just as a rule, but as a gift—a day of rest, reflection, and connection with Him.

God's desire for relationship is seen throughout Scripture. In Jeremiah 31:33, God says, *"I will be their God, and they will be my people."* He wants closeness, not cold religion. The Ten Commandments show that God wants our hearts, not just our obedience.

7. God is Moral and Defines Right from Wrong

Each of the Ten Commandments reveals that God has a moral standard. He is not morally neutral or silent—He defines what is good and what is evil. Unlike man-made standards that shift with culture, God's laws are rooted in His unchanging character. Malachi 3:6 says, *"I the Lord do not change."*

The Bible, as a whole, reinforces this. It teaches that God is righteous, just, merciful, holy, loving, and true—and His commandments reflect those attributes.

Final Thoughts

The Ten Commandments are more than rules—they are a portrait of God's character. They show us that God is holy, truthful, faithful, just, compassionate, and relational. And when we read them alongside the rest of the Bible, we begin to understand the kind of God we serve—not a distant lawgiver, but a loving Father who desires relationship, obedience, and transformation. To know the Ten Commandments is to begin to know the heart of God. And to know the Bible is to discover His character revealed page after page.

Taking Action

Think | Write | Grow

Based on what you learned in this chapter:

What's something you will stop doing or a habit you will break?

_____

_____

What's something you will start doing or a habit you will create?

_____

_____

What's the potential positive impact of improving in this area?

_____

_____

Chapter Twenty-Seven

There Is Power in Fellowship

Rival 4: Ignorance

I n a world increasingly marked by individualism, isolation, and digital substitutes for human connection, Christian fellowship and regular church attendance remain powerful and essential parts of the Christian life. While personal prayer and private study of God's Word are vital, there is a unique and God-ordained power in gathering with other believers—not just occasionally, but consistently.

The early Church understood this deeply. Acts 2:42 says, *"They devoted themselves to the apostles' teaching and to fellowship, to the breaking of bread and to prayer."* Their devotion to one another was not a casual social arrangement—it was a spiritual priority. Today, the same truth holds: there is life-changing strength in Christian community.

Here are five biblical and practical reasons why there is power in Christian fellowship and attending church together:

1. We Experience God's Presence in a Unique Way

Jesus said in Matthew 18:20, *"For where two or three gather in my name, there am I with them."* While God is always present with us individually, there is a special manifestation of His presence when believers gather in unity. In corporate worship, prayer, and teaching, we often sense God's nearness in a way that is different from when we are alone.

The early Church saw miracles, healings, and bold faith emerge from its shared gatherings. The same power is available today when believers come together with expectation and hunger for God's presence.

2. Fellowship Provides Encouragement and Accountability

Hebrews 10:24–25 exhorts us, *"Let us consider how we may spur one another on toward love and good deeds, not giving up meeting together... but encouraging one another."* Life is hard. Faith is tested. Temptations are real. And no one was meant to walk this journey alone.

Christian fellowship allows us to strengthen each other, pray for one another, share burdens, and speak life into discouraging moments. It also provides accountability—loving correction and support that keeps us from drifting away from the truth or growing spiritually cold. Iron sharpens iron (Proverbs 27:17), and we need people in our lives who will challenge, stretch, and build us up in Christ.

3. Spiritual Gifts Are Meant to Be Shared

1 Corinthians 12:7 tells us, *"Now to each one the manifestation of the Spirit is given for the common good."* Every believer has been given spiritual gifts—not to be hoarded, but to serve and edify the Body of Christ. These gifts find their greatest purpose when exercised in the context of fellowship and local church life.

Whether it's teaching, encouragement, hospitality, prophecy, worship, or administration—your gift was designed to bless others. When we isolate ourselves, we deprive the Church of the unique contribution God has placed in us. And we, in turn, miss out on the gifts others have that we desperately need.

4. We Reflect the Unity and Diversity of the Body of Christ

The Church is called the Body of Christ—not a collection of disconnected individuals, but a living, breathing, unified body with many parts (1 Corinthians 12:12–27). Attending church and engaging in Christian fellowship reminds us that we're part of something much bigger than ourselves.

In a world marked by division, the Church should be a testimony of supernatural unity. People of different backgrounds, cultures, ages, and experiences coming together under one name—Jesus—is a powerful witness to the world. This kind of unity isn't found anywhere else. It reflects the heart of God and the future of eternity.

5. Together, We Advance the Mission of the Gospel

Jesus didn't send His disciples out alone. He sent them two by two (Mark 6:7). Likewise, the early Church grew rapidly because it worked together to evangelize, disciple, and serve. The Great Commission was not given to individuals in isolation—it was given to the Church.

When we gather regularly, we become equipped and empowered to go out. The church is not a social club or a weekly event—it is the launchpad for mission. We are reminded of our purpose, aligned with God's vision, and sent out into the world as ambassadors of Christ.

Final Thoughts

Christian fellowship and attending church aren't just traditions—they are channels of God's power, presence, and purpose. They guard us from spiritual drift, strengthen us in hardship, grow our gifts, and connect us to the larger body of Christ. In a world that says, "Do it yourself," God's Word says, "Do it together." If you've drifted from church or underestimated the value of Christian community, now is the time to return. The strength, joy, and purpose you're longing for may not be missing from your heart—but from your fellowship. There is power in gathering. There is power in unity. And there is power in the Church—because God designed it that way.

Taking Action

Think | Write | Grow

Based on what you learned in this chapter:

What's something you will stop doing or a habit you will break?

_____

_____

What's something you will start doing or a habit you will create?

_____

_____

What's the potential positive impact of improving in this area?

_____

_____

Chapter Twenty-Eight

God's Word Is Best as a Journey

Rival 4: Ignorance

T he Bible is the most powerful and life-changing book in history. But for a new believer, it can also feel overwhelming. With 66 books, over 1,000 chapters, and a wide range of writing styles—from history and poetry to prophecy and doctrine—many Christians don't know where to start. They want to grow in faith but feel intimidated by the size and complexity of Scripture.

The good news is this: you don't need to understand everything all at once to start growing. God didn't give us the Bible to confuse us, but to draw us into a deeper relationship with Him. With a simple and systematic approach, any new believer can learn the most essential parts of the Bible—and lay a strong foundation for lifelong growth.

Here's a step-by-step guide that removes the pressure and makes Bible learning accessible, meaningful, and even exciting.

Step 1: Start with the Gospels (Matthew, Mark, Luke, and John)

If you're new to the Bible, begin with the life of Jesus. The Gospels—Matthew, Mark, Luke, and John—tell the story of His birth, ministry, death, and resurrection. Everything in the Bible points to Jesus, so starting with His life gives you the clearest picture of who God is and what the Christian life is all about.

Start with the book of John. It's simple, powerful, and focuses heavily on who Jesus is and why He came. Then, move to Mark, which is fast-paced and action-oriented. From there, you can explore Matthew and Luke for more teaching and background.

Tip: As you read, write down questions, key verses, and what stands out. Don't rush. Let the words sink in.

Step 2: Learn the Big Story (Genesis, Exodus, Psalms, Proverbs)

After the Gospels, step back and look at how it all began. Genesis introduces you to creation, the fall of man, and God's first promises of redemption. It helps explain why we need Jesus.

Exodus tells the story of God rescuing His people and giving the Ten Commandments. It introduces major themes like freedom, covenant, and worship.

Psalms is a book of prayers and praise—perfect for learning how to talk to God honestly. Proverbs is filled with short, practical wisdom for everyday life.

By reading these books, you begin to see how God's plan unfolds from the beginning and how He interacts with people just like you.

Step 3: Get Grounded in Faith (Romans, Ephesians, James)

Once you've read about Jesus and the foundations of faith, it's helpful to understand what it means to live as a Christian. The letters (also called epistles) in the New Testament explain how to follow Jesus daily.

Start with Romans, which is a deep but powerful book about salvation, grace, and the purpose of the Gospel. Then, read Ephesians to understand your identity in Christ. James is also great for practical, everyday guidance.

These books will help you build a solid understanding of what you believe and how it applies to real life.

Step 4: Make a Habit (Read a Little Each Day)

You don't need to read the whole Bible in a month to grow. In fact, growth happens best through consistency. Try reading a chapter a day or using a Bible reading plan that guides you through key parts of Scripture.

Consider starting a journal to reflect on what you read. Ask three simple questions:

- What does this teach me about God?

- What does this teach me about myself?

- How can I apply this today?

Also, pray before and after you read. Ask God to open your eyes and help you understand.

Step 5: Stay Connected (Join a Bible Study or Church Group)

Learning the Bible is not meant to be done in isolation. Find a local church or small group where you can ask questions, hear teaching, and discuss what you're learning. God often uses others to confirm His truth and help you grow.

Even joining an online Bible study or watching a trusted pastor's teaching series can provide structure and encouragement as you grow.

Final Thoughts

The Bible may seem big, but it's not meant to be intimidating—it's meant to be transforming. You don't need to master it overnight. What matters most is starting with a willing heart and taking one step at a time. Begin with Jesus. Learn the big picture. Ground yourself in the truth. Be consistent. Stay connected. God doesn't expect you to know everything—He simply invites you to walk with Him and let His Word shape your life day by day. Over time, you'll not only understand the Bible more clearly—you'll love it more deeply. Remember that you're not reading to impress God—you're reading to know Him. And that's where true growth begins.

Taking Action

Think | Write | Grow

Based on what you learned in this chapter:

What's something you will stop doing or a habit you will break?

_____

_____

What's something you will start doing or a habit you will create?

_____

_____

What's the potential positive impact of improving in this area?

_____

_____

RIVAL 5

---◆---

PAST HURTS

"Accept God's Grace"

Chapter Twenty-Nine

Nobody's Perfect, Especially the Church

Rival 5: Past Hurts

For many people, the word "church" once meant comfort, community, and connection with God. But for others, that same word now brings up feelings of betrayal, judgment, and disappointment. The truth is, not all who leave the church are running from God. Some are running from pain caused by hypocrites, toxic leadership, or unhealthy church cultures. In far too many cases, bad churches and inconsistent Christians have caused good people to walk away.

If that's your story, you're not alone. Your hurt is real, and your caution is valid. But the God who calls His people to gather has *not* abandoned the church—and neither should we, if we desire to heal and grow. The key is learning how to re-approach church life slowly, wisely, and with renewed purpose.

Why People Leave: The Wounds of Church Hurt

The Bible teaches that the church is the Body of Christ (1 Corinthians 12:27), a place of worship, fellowship, and spiritual growth. But when people experience the *opposite*—such as gossip instead of grace, control instead of compassion, or abuse instead of accountability—they begin to question whether the church is worth attending at all.

Here are some of the most common reasons good-hearted people leave church:

- Hypocrisy: Seeing leaders preach one thing but live another.

- Judgemental attitudes: Being shamed for struggling instead of being helped to heal.

- Spiritual manipulation: Leadership using Scripture to guilt, control, or elevate themselves.

- Exclusion: Feeling like an outsider because of background, appearance, or past mistakes.

- Moral failure by church leaders: Discovering that someone trusted was living a double life.

Sadly, these experiences leave many feeling disillusioned not just with church, but with *God Himself*. The danger is that people confuse God's perfection with man's imperfection. But while churches may fail, God never does.

God Still Values the Church

Despite human failure, the church is still God's idea. Scripture tells us to *"not give up meeting together"* (Hebrews 10:25) and describes the church as the bride of Christ (Ephesians 5:25–27). Jesus died to redeem people and bring them into community—not just with Him, but with one another.

Rejecting every church because of a bad one is like rejecting medicine because of a bad doctor. The goal is not to walk away entirely, but to heal, recover, and re-engage—at a healthy pace, with the right focus.

Steps to Begin Going to Church Again—Slowly and Safely

If you've been hurt by the church and feel distant from community, here are five gentle, grace-filled steps to help you begin the journey back:

1. Give Yourself Permission to Heal

Healing takes time, and it's okay to admit that church hurt you. Don't bury it. Talk to God about it honestly. You might also benefit from processing with a trusted Christian counselor or mentor who understands spiritual trauma. Remember, acknowledging the pain is not bitterness—it's the beginning of freedom.

2. Separate God From the People Who Misrepresented Him

People may have misused God's name, but that doesn't mean God approved of their actions. Ask God to reveal *His true character* to you again through His Word. He is not a hypocrite, manipulator, or abuser. He is just, merciful, and faithful. Let your relationship with God lead you back to His people—not the other way around.

3. Research and Visit Churches Quietly

Take your time. Look for churches that are known for biblical teaching, authentic worship, servant-hearted leadership, and a grace-filled community. Read the church's mission and beliefs online. Watch their services virtually, if available. When you're ready, attend quietly without pressure to join anything immediately.

Observe how people interact. Are they welcoming without being pushy? Is the message grounded in Scripture or centered on personality? Healthy churches don't demand your trust—they earn it over time.

4. Start Small and Be Honest With God

You don't have to jump into every program or volunteer role. Start by attending a Sunday service. If that feels like too much, start with a small group or midweek Bible study. Let your re-entry be gradual and guided by God's peace.

Ask Him each week: *"God, what's my next step?"* He will lead you gently. The goal is not to check a box—it's to rebuild your spiritual life in community.

5. Focus on Jesus, Not Perfection

No church is perfect. But a good church will humbly acknowledge that and aim to reflect Christ as best it can. Don't let a search for perfection keep you from genuine fellowship. Keep your eyes on Jesus—not on the mistakes of man.

As you re-enter church life, remember: you are not going back to a building—you are returning to a God-designed community that, despite its flaws, is part of your spiritual growth and healing.

Final Thoughts

Church hurt is real. But so is the healing power of God's presence within a healthy church community. Bad experiences don't have to define your faith journey forever. With grace, wisdom, and patience, you can take small steps back into fellowship and rediscover the strength, love, and encouragement that come from gathering with God's people. You don't have to rush. Just start. Healing doesn't happen all at once—but it begins with one step toward home.

Taking Action

Think | Write | Grow

Based on what you learned in this chapter:

What's something you will stop doing or a habit you will break?

_____

_____

What's something you will start doing or a habit you will create?

_____

_____

What's the potential positive impact of improving in this area?

_____

_____

Chapter Thirty

Unanswered Prayer Isn't Ignored Prayer

Rival 5: Past Hurts

At some point in life, every believer wrestles with the weight of an unanswered prayer. Whether it's a healing that never came, a relationship that wasn't restored, a door that remained closed, or a plea for help that seemed to be met with silence, the pain of waiting—or worse, the feeling of being ignored—can be deeply discouraging. In those moments, it's tempting to draw conclusions about God's goodness, His power, or His love. But here's the truth: unanswered prayers are not proof of God's absence, indifference, or failure. And they are never a reason to give up on Him.

Though we may not always understand God's timing or reasoning, Scripture reminds us over and over again that He is faithful, wise, and working—even when we cannot see it. Rather than walking away in disappointment, we must learn to trust deeper and wait longer, believing that unanswered prayers are not unanswered lives.

1. God Sees What We Cannot See

Our perspective is limited. We see only the present moment, the pain we're in, and the desire we're holding onto. But God sees the beginning from the end. Isaiah 55:8–9 says, *"For my thoughts are not your thoughts, neither are your ways my ways," declares the Lord. "As the heavens are higher than the earth, so are my ways higher than your ways and my thoughts than your thoughts."*

Sometimes God says "no" or "not yet," not because He doesn't care, but because He knows what we cannot see. He sees the long-term consequences, the bigger picture, the spiritual maturity that will come through the waiting, or even the protection hidden in the delay. What feels like divine silence may actually be a divine strategy.

2. God Is Not a Vending Machine—He Is a Father

We often approach prayer with a transactional mindset: "If I pray hard enough, believe strongly enough, and do the right things, God will give me what I ask." But God isn't a cosmic vending machine. He is a loving Father, and like any good parent, He sometimes withholds what we ask for because He's working toward something better.

Jesus said in Matthew 7:9–11, *"Which of you, if your son asks for bread, will give him a stone?... If you then, though you are evil, know how to give good gifts to your children, how much more will your Father in heaven give good gifts to those who ask him!"*

If we trust God's love, we must also trust His *decisions*. A "no" or "wait" from God is not rejection—it is a response shaped by His perfect knowledge and perfect love.

3. Even Jesus Faced Unanswered Prayers

In the Garden of Gethsemane, Jesus prayed with great anguish: *"Father, if it is possible, let this cup pass from me."* (Matthew 26:39). Yet, the answer was "no." Not because God didn't love Jesus—but because through that "no," the greatest redemption in history was made possible.

Jesus trusted the Father enough to surrender, saying, *"Yet not as I will, but as you will."* This is the model of faith we are called to follow. Even when the answer hurts, even when it costs everything—God's will is still good.

4. Unanswered Prayers Can Deepen Our Faith

Often, it's not the prayers that get answered instantly that grow our faith—but the ones that go unanswered and teach us how to endure, surrender, and trust. Waiting purifies our motives, builds our character, and draws us closer to the heart of God.

Romans 5:3–4 says, *"We also glory in our sufferings, because we know that suffering produces perseverance; perseverance, character; and character, hope."*

God uses every season of silence to shape something in us that easy answers never could.

5. God Is Always Working Behind the Scenes

Just because we don't see immediate results doesn't mean God isn't at work. Sometimes, He is working in hearts, arranging circumstances, or preparing us to receive what we asked for. Other times, He is shifting our desires so that we begin to pray differently and more in alignment with His will.

Ephesians 3:20 promises that God *"is able to do immeasurably more than all we ask or imagine, according to* His *power that is at work within us."* That power is still active—even when the answer hasn't come.

Final Thoughts

Unanswered prayer is not a reason to give up on God. It's a reason to lean in, dig deeper, and remind ourselves of who He is—even when life doesn't make sense. God has not forgotten you. His silence is not absence. His delay is not denial. His plan is still good, even when it's hidden. Don't judge God based on the chapter you're in—He's still writing the story. And one day, you'll look back and see that even the unanswered prayers were part of His perfect, loving plan. Until then, hold on to faith. Keep praying. Keep trusting. And don't give up on the God who will never give up on you.

Taking Action

Think | Write | Grow

Based on what you learned in this chapter:

What's something you will stop doing or a habit you will break?

_____

_____

What's something you will start doing or a habit you will create?

_____

_____

What's the potential positive impact of improving in this area?

_____

_____

Chapter Thirty-One

Bad Things Happen to Good People

Rival 5: Past Hurts

F ew questions trouble the human heart more than this: Why do bad things happen to good people? From personal tragedies to global suffering, Christians often wrestle with the mystery of pain in a world created by a good and powerful God. It's not just a theological question—it's an emotional and deeply personal one.

Why does the kind, faithful woman battle cancer while the corrupt seem to thrive? Why does a loving family lose their child in a tragic accident? Why do godly people suffer betrayal, loss, and heartache while others who mock God appear untouched?

This tension is not new. The Bible doesn't avoid it—in fact, it addresses it head-on. And while it may not give us *every* answer, it gives us enough to trust God even when life hurts.

1. We Live in a Broken World

The first and most foundational truth Scripture teaches is that we live in a fallen world. When Adam and Eve sinned in the Garden of Eden, sin entered creation—and with it came pain, disease, injustice, and death. Romans 5:12 says, *"Sin entered the world through one man, and death through sin, and in this way death came to all people."*

This means that bad things don't always happen as a direct result of someone's choices. Sometimes, it's simply the result of living in a world that is not as God originally designed it to be. Until Christ returns and restores all things, we will continue to experience the consequences of sin—even when we ourselves are walking in righteousness.

2. God Never Promised a Pain-Free Life

One of the biggest misunderstandings Christians can have is the belief that following Jesus guarantees protection from hardship. While God promises His presence, His comfort, and His peace, He never promises a life without suffering.

In fact, Jesus warned us of the opposite. In John 16:33, He said, *"In this world you will have trouble. But take heart! I have overcome the world."* The Apostle Paul, who lived a faithful and sacrificial life, endured beatings, imprisonments, and hardships. Being "good" by God's standards has never guaranteed a life free of pain.

3. God Uses Suffering for Greater Purposes

Though suffering is not good, God can use it for good. Romans 8:28 reminds us, *"And we know that in all things God works for the good of those who love him, who have been called according to his purpose."* This doesn't mean every situation will feel good or make sense in the moment, but it means that nothing is wasted in God's hands.

Through suffering, God often deepens our character, builds perseverance, purifies our faith, and helps us minister to others with greater compassion. Trials can strip away superficial comforts and draw us into a more intimate relationship with God.

James 1:2–4 even tells us to *"consider it pure joy... whenever you face trials of many kinds, because you know that the testing of your faith produces perseverance."*

4. God Understands Our Suffering—Because He Suffered Too

The Christian God is not distant or indifferent to pain. He entered into it. Jesus, the Son of God, experienced betrayal, rejection, poverty, torture, and death. Isaiah 53:3 calls Him *"a man of sorrows, familiar with suffering."*

On the cross, Jesus bore the full weight of humanity's sin and pain—not because He deserved it, but because He chose to suffer in our place. Because of this, we don't serve a God who merely observes our pain—we serve One who walked through it, overcame it, and now walks with us in it.

5. This Life Is Not the End of the Story

When bad things happen, we often feel like injustice is winning. But Scripture reminds us that this life is not the whole story. There will be a day when every tear is wiped away, every wrong is made right, and every injustice is judged by the righteous King.

Revelation 21:4 promises, *"He will wipe every tear from their eyes. There will be no more death or mourning or crying or pain."* For the believer, our hope is not in this life being perfect, but in the eternal life that Christ has secured for us.

Final Thoughts

Yes, bad things happen to good people—but the Bible shows us why, and it gives us hope in the middle of our pain. We live in a broken world, but we serve a faithful God. He doesn't always explain everything, but He promises to be with us through everything. So, when life hurts and answers feel far away, don't turn from God—run to Him. He is not the cause of your suffering, but the One who redeems it. He is your refuge, your healer, your hope, and your ultimate victory. God may not always change your circumstances, but He will always use them to change you—for your good and His glory.

Taking Action

Think | Write | Grow

Based on what you learned in this chapter:

What's something you will stop doing or a habit you will break?

_____

_____

What's something you will start doing or a habit you will create?

_____

_____

What's the potential positive impact of improving in this area?

_____

_____

Chapter Thirty-Two

It's Okay to be Angry at God

Rival 5: Past Hurts

It's a struggle many believers face but few openly admit: being angry with God. When life falls apart, when prayers go unanswered, or when suffering seems unfair, it's easy to start pointing the finger upward. In the middle of loss, betrayal, sickness, or disappointment, you may find yourself asking, *"Why did God let this happen?"* or even *"God, where were You?"*

This anger can quietly grow into resentment, and that resentment can cause distance in your relationship with God. But here's the truth: God can handle your honesty, and He desires to heal your heart—not condemn it. If you're carrying anger or blame toward God, there is a path toward peace, reconciliation, and spiritual restoration.

Here are six biblical and practical steps you can take to begin releasing your anger and drawing close to God again:

1. Acknowledge Your Emotions Honestly

The first step to healing is admitting that you're hurt, confused, or angry. Don't pretend to be okay or spiritualize your pain. God already knows what you feel. In fact, some of the Bible's most faithful people—like David, Job, and Jeremiah—expressed deep frustration and even anger toward God.

David cried out in Psalm 13:1, *"How long, O Lord? Will you forget me forever?"* Job questioned God repeatedly through suffering. God never condemned them for their honesty—instead, He drew near.

God isn't afraid of your questions. He welcomes your honesty. Pour out your emotions in prayer. Journal your thoughts. Let it all out. This is the beginning of healing.

2. Remind Yourself of Who God Is—Not Just What You Feel

When we're angry, our emotions can cloud our perspective. We start defining God by our pain instead of His promises. But Scripture is filled with truth that anchors us when feelings become overwhelming.

Psalm 145:8 says, *"The Lord is gracious and compassionate, slow to anger and rich in love."* Just because life feels cruel doesn't mean God is. He is still faithful, still loving, and still in control—even when we don't understand what He's doing.

Reading the Bible helps shift your focus from what you're feeling to what is true. Rehearse God's faithfulness in the past. Meditate on His character. Let His Word speak louder than your wounds.

3. Differentiate Between What God Allowed and What God Caused

Many times, anger toward God stems from confusion about His role in our suffering. While God is sovereign, that doesn't mean He causes every painful event. We live in a broken world, affected by sin, free will, and spiritual warfare.

God sometimes permits suffering, but He never delights in it (Lamentations 3:33). He may allow trials for reasons we can't yet see—to strengthen our faith, refine our character, or accomplish greater purposes.

It's okay to wrestle with this tension, but don't let a limited understanding lead to a distorted view of God's heart. He grieves with you. He's for you, not against you.

4. Surrender the Right to Understand Everything

One of the hardest, but most freeing, things you can do is to surrender the need to have all the answers. Proverbs 3:5 reminds us to *"Trust in the Lord with all your heart and lean not on your own understanding."*

Faith doesn't mean pretending to understand. It means choosing to trust, even when you don't. Like Job, who after questioning God was humbled by God's greatness, we may never receive a clear "why"—but we can rest in who God is.

Let go of the demand for perfect clarity and open your hands to receive peace instead.

5. Let God Heal You, Not Just Explain Things to You

Sometimes we want explanations, but what we really need is healing. Your anger might be masking grief, disappointment, or unprocessed trauma. God is more concerned with healing your heart than satisfying your curiosity.

Psalm 34:18 says, *"The Lord is close to the brokenhearted and saves those who are crushed in spirit."* Invite Him into your brokenness. Allow His Spirit to comfort you, speak to you, and restore your trust.

God doesn't just want to fix your pain—He wants to walk with you through it.

6. Rebuild the Relationship One Step at a Time

Restoring your relationship with God doesn't have to happen overnight. Take small steps. Talk to Him daily, even if your prayers feel awkward. Read a few verses of Scripture. Listen to worship music. Join a trusted community or talk to a spiritual mentor.

Think of it like rebuilding trust after a storm—steady, slow, and sincere. As you take one step toward God, you'll begin to experience His grace meeting you in surprising ways.

James 4:8 says, *"Draw near to God, and he will draw near to you."* You don't have to come perfectly—just come honestly.

Final Thoughts

Being angry with God doesn't make you a bad Christian—it makes you human. But staying angry and blaming Him without pursuing healing will rob you of the peace, hope, and intimacy He wants to give you. God isn't finished with your story. He hasn't walked away. In fact, He's the one holding out

His hand, waiting for you to return—not with polished prayers, but with a surrendered heart. Let today be the day you stop blaming God—and start trusting Him again, one step at a time.

Taking Action

Think | Write | Grow

Based on what you learned in this chapter:

What's something you will stop doing or a habit you will break?

_____

_____

What's something you will start doing or a habit you will create?

_____

_____

What's the potential positive impact of improving in this area?

_____

_____

Chapter Thirty-Three

God Understands Your Pain

Rival 5: Past Hurts

P ain and loss have a way of shaking us to our core. When we lose a loved one, endure heartbreak, or suffer through disappointment, it can feel like our relationship with God begins to fracture. Grief can lead to doubt. Silence can feel like abandonment. And unanswered questions can cause us to pull away from the One we once trusted.

If you've found yourself feeling distant from God after a season of suffering, you're not alone—and you're not beyond healing. God is not offended by your pain, nor is He finished with you. In fact, Scripture shows that He is closest to the brokenhearted (Psalm 34:18). The good news is that no matter how far you've drifted, God is always ready to restore what's been lost between you and Him.

Here are six biblical and practical steps to help you restore your relationship with God after pain and loss:

1. Be Honest With God About Your Pain

God doesn't want a polished performance—He wants a genuine relationship. If you're angry, confused, numb, or heartbroken, say so. He can handle your raw emotions.

Many faithful people in the Bible expressed deep sorrow to God. David cried, *"How long, Lord? Will you forget me forever?"* (Psalm 13:1). Job poured out his grief and frustration. Even Jesus wept and cried out to the Father in agony. These honest expressions weren't signs of weak faith—they were acts of trust.

God would rather hear your honest cries than your silent withdrawal.

2. Stop Blaming God and Start Trusting His Heart

It's natural to wonder *why* painful things happen. But if we stay stuck in blaming God, it becomes a barrier to healing. While we may never fully understand the "why," we must remember the "Who"—a God who is good, sovereign, and compassionate, even in our confusion.

Romans 8:28 doesn't say everything *is* good, but that *"in all things, God works for the good of those who love him."* Even in pain, God is weaving redemption, growth, and eternal purpose.

Letting go of blame doesn't mean denying your pain—it means choosing to trust that God's character is still faithful, even when life isn't fair.

3. Rebuild Spiritual Habits—One Step at a Time

When pain enters our lives, it's easy to stop praying, reading the Bible, or engaging in church. And while space to grieve is necessary, spiritual disconnection can cause our hearts to grow cold over time.

Start rebuilding small spiritual habits, even if they feel difficult at first:

- Read a few verses of Scripture each day.

- Pray simply: *"God, help me find my way back to You."*

- Listen to worship music.

- Journal your thoughts and emotions.

- Attend a church service or small group.

You don't need to feel everything to start—you just need to take one step forward. Healing begins with showing up again in faith, even when it hurts.

4. Surround Yourself With Truth and Community

When you're hurting, the enemy loves to isolate you and whisper lies: *"God doesn't care about you. You're alone. Your faith is broken."* To counter those lies, you need truth—and people who will speak it over you.

Find a Christ-centered community where it's safe to grieve, ask questions, and be supported. Share your story with someone mature in faith. Let others pray for you when you can't pray for yourself.

Galatians 6:2 says, *"Carry each other's burdens, and in this way you will fulfill the law of Christ."* God often restores us through His people.

5. Focus on God's Presence, Not Just His Answers

In times of loss, we often want explanations—but God offers something better: Himself. The comfort you long for isn't found in understanding the past—it's found in encountering God's presence in the present.

When Moses asked God for reassurance in the wilderness, God responded, *"My presence will go with you, and I will give you rest"* (Exodus 33:14).

Don't wait for every answer before reconnecting with God. Seek His presence—through prayer, worship, and stillness—and you'll find the peace your heart truly needs.

6. Believe That Restoration Is Possible—Because God Is a Restorer

God specializes in restoration. He doesn't just mend broken hearts—He makes them new. Joel 2:25 says, *"I will restore to you the years that the locust has eaten."* That's God's promise to take what was lost, stolen, or broken and use it for your good and His glory.

You may feel spiritually dry or emotionally numb today, but God can bring beauty from ashes (Isaiah 61:3). He is patient, gracious, and always ready to welcome you back with open arms—just like the father did in the Parable of the Prodigal Son.

Final Thoughts

Pain and loss may have created distance between you and God, but they don't have to define your relationship with Him. Restoration is not about going back to where you were—it's about growing into something deeper, stronger, and more personal than before. Take a deep breath. Let go of guilt. Reach out in honesty. God hasn't moved—He's been with you the whole time. Now is the time to return. Not with perfect faith, but with a willing heart. God is ready to meet you in your pain and walk with you toward healing.

Taking Action

Think | Write | Grow

Based on what you learned in this chapter:

What's something you will stop doing or a habit you will break?

_____

_____

What's something you will start doing or a habit you will create?

_____

_____

What's the potential positive impact of improving in this area?

_____

_____

Chapter Thirty-Four

God Sees Past Your Mistakes

Rival 5: Past Hurts

One of the heaviest burdens a Christian can carry is the weight of past mistakes, shame, and guilt. Even after coming to faith, many believers still wrestle with a lingering sense of failure—replaying regrets, hiding brokenness, and wondering if God has truly forgiven them.

If you've ever asked, *"How could God still love me after what I've done?"* or *"Will He ever look at me the same again?"*—you're not alone. But the heart of the Gospel is not about punishment, it's about reconciliation. God doesn't just forgive you—He restores you. And He wants you to walk in freedom, not shame.

Here's a biblical and practical roadmap for reconciling with God after failure:

1. Come to God Honestly—Don't Hide

Guilt often makes us want to run from God, like Adam and Eve did in the Garden. But hiding never leads to healing. Reconciliation begins with honest confession—coming before God with your full truth.

1 John 1:9 promises: *"If we confess our sins, He is faithful and just and will forgive us our sins and purify us from all unrighteousness."*

Don't minimize your sin or pretend it didn't happen—but don't wallow in it either. God already knows. He's just waiting for you to come with a humble heart.

2. Accept God's Forgiveness by Faith, Not Feeling

Forgiveness is not based on how you *feel*—it's based on what God has already *done*. Through Jesus's death and resurrection, your debt has been paid in full. You don't need to earn God's love or try to "make it up" to Him.

Romans 8:1 reminds us: *"There is now no condemnation for those who are in Christ Jesus."*

Even if you still feel guilty, the truth is this: if you've confessed and repented, you are forgiven. Trust God's Word more than your emotions.

3. Release the Shame—You Are Not Your Past

Guilt says, *"I did something bad."* Shame says, *"I am bad."*

But as a child of God, your identity is not found in your past sins—it's found in Christ. You are redeemed, forgiven, and made new.

2 Corinthians 5:17 says: *"If anyone is in Christ, he is a new creation. The old has gone, the new is here!"*

To reconcile with God, you must stop labeling yourself by what you've done and start embracing who He says you are.

4. Understand That God Uses Brokenness

Your past mistakes don't disqualify you—they can actually become the very thing God uses to display His grace and reach others. Some of the most powerful people in Scripture—David, Paul, Peter—made terrible mistakes. But their stories didn't end in failure. God used their brokenness to bring glory to Himself.

Romans 8:28 assures us: *"And we know that in all things God works for the good of those who love him."*

God is not surprised by your failures. In His mercy, He can bring purpose from your past and healing from your pain.

5. Take Steps Toward Restoring Intimacy

Reconciliation isn't just about being forgiven—it's about restoring relationship. Like a broken friendship that's healed over time, your closeness with God can be rebuilt. How?

- Spend time in prayer—even if it's messy.

- Open your Bible daily and let truth reshape your thoughts.

- Worship—not just in song, but with your whole life.

- Surround yourself with believers who encourage your growth.

James 4:8 says: *"Draw near to God, and He will draw near to you."*

God isn't waiting for perfection—He's waiting for *you*.

6. Forgive Yourself Because God Has

One of the hardest steps for many believers is forgiving themselves. But if God—the holy, righteous Judge—has chosen to forgive you, who are you to keep holding it against yourself?

To forgive yourself doesn't mean you forget—it means you stop punishing yourself for what Jesus already paid for. It means choosing freedom over self-condemnation.

7. Walk in the Light and Let Grace Transform You

Shame thrives in secrecy. One of the most powerful ways to overcome guilt is by walking in the light—being open with God and trustworthy people.

Find a mentor, pastor, or close Christian friend you can share your journey with. Healing accelerates when you stop hiding and let others walk with you.

Ephesians 5:8 says: *"For you were once darkness, but now you are light in the Lord. Live as children of light."*

Let God's grace change you from the inside out—and let your story be a testimony of His mercy.

Final Thoughts

Reconciliation with God is not earned—it's received. Jesus didn't come to shame sinners—He came to save them. Whatever you've done, however far you've drifted, you can return. God is not angry at you—He's longing to welcome you back. Lay down the guilt. Release the shame. Embrace the grace. And start again today—healed, restored, and deeply loved.

Taking Action

Think | Write | Grow

Based on what you learned in this chapter:

What's something you will stop doing or a habit you will break?

_____

_____

What's something you will start doing or a habit you will create?

_____

_____

What's the potential positive impact of improving in this area?

_____

_____

Chapter Thirty-Five

Run the Race Marked Out for You

Rival 5: Past Hurts

T he Christian life is often compared to a race—not a sprint of quick success, but a marathon of steady perseverance. This imagery, drawn from Scripture, captures the reality of what it means to follow Jesus faithfully through seasons of both joy and hardship. Hebrews 12:1–2 gives us a clear and powerful command: *"Let us run with endurance the race that is set before us, fixing our eyes on Jesus, the author and perfecter of our faith."*

But what does it truly mean to "run the race," and how do we do it not with weariness or dread, but with joy?

To run the race set before us means to embrace the life God has uniquely called us to live, marked by purpose, discipline, and unwavering focus on Christ. It's about pressing forward through trials, temptations, and distractions—knowing that there is an eternal reward ahead. And it's not about running in your own strength, but running *with* God, *for* God, and *toward* God.

1. Understand That the Race Is Personal and Purposeful

The phrase "the race that is set before us" reminds us that each believer has a specific course—designed and allowed by God. Your race may look different from someone else's, and that's okay. God does not compare you to others; He calls you to be faithful to your assignment.

Ephesians 2:10 says, *"For we are God's handiwork, created in Christ Jesus to do good works, which God prepared in advance for us to do."* That means your journey—your victories, your struggles, your calling—is not an accident. You're running a God-ordained race, and He's equipped you for it.

Knowing your race has purpose gives it meaning, even in the hard moments. It also keeps you from falling into the trap of comparison. Stay in your lane. Run *your* race.

2. Lay Aside Every Weight and Sin

Hebrews 12:1 starts with a vital instruction: *"Let us throw off everything that hinders and the sin that so easily entangles."* Just as a runner must shed anything that slows them down, so too must the Christian lay aside burdens, distractions, and sins that hold them back.

Weights aren't always sinful things—they might be distractions, unhealthy habits, unresolved bitterness, or even good things that are keeping you from God's best. Sin, on the other hand, will entangle your feet, cloud your judgment, and weaken your endurance.

To run freely, you must run light. Ask God regularly, *"What am I carrying that You never asked me to?"* Then let it go. Fix your eyes on Jesus.

The center of our race is not performance—it's a Person. Hebrews 12:2 calls Jesus *"the author and perfecter of our faith."* He is both the starting line and the finish line. He began your faith journey, and He will carry it to completion (Philippians 1:6).

Fixing your eyes on Jesus means making Him your focus—not your failures, not your feelings, not other people. When you lock eyes with the Savior, your perspective shifts. You're reminded of why you started. You gain strength from His example. And you learn to run not for approval, but from a place of love and identity.

4. Endure with Joy, Not Just Duty

Endurance is essential—but so is joy. Too many Christians are running their race with gritted teeth, full of anxiety, or burnout. But Scripture tells us Jesus Himself endured the cross *"for the joy set before him"* (Hebrews 12:2). That means He didn't just suffer—He did so with hope, purpose, and joy in what was to come.

We, too, can run with joy when we remember what lies ahead: deeper intimacy with Christ, the transformation of our character, and the eternal reward of hearing, *"Well done, good and faithful servant."*

Joy doesn't mean the race will be easy. It means we run with a confidence that our suffering is not wasted, and our Savior is with us.

5. Stay Encouraged by the Cloud of Witnesses

Hebrews 12:1 opens by reminding us that we are *"surrounded by such a great cloud of witnesses."* These are the heroes of faith from Hebrews 11—Abraham, Moses, Ruth, and many others who endured great trials and still finished well.

Their stories remind us that we're not alone. They're proof that it's possible to run faithfully, even in hardship. And their legacy challenges us to keep going.

You may stumble. You may get tired. But the same God who sustained them will sustain you.

Final Thoughts

Running the race set before you as a Christian is about faithful endurance, daily surrender, and joyful perseverance. It's about letting go of everything that weighs you down and focusing on the One who ran ahead of you and made a way. The race is not won by speed, but by faithfulness. And the reward is not just in the finish—it's in walking closely with Jesus every step of the way. So keep running. Run with purpose. Run with joy. And run, knowing that the One who called you is running beside you, cheering you on until the very end. Because the finish line is worth every step.

Taking Action

Think | Write | Grow

Based on what you learned in this chapter:

What's something you will stop doing or a habit you will break?

_____

_____

What's something you will start doing or a habit you will create?

_____

_____

What's the potential positive impact of improving in this area?

_____

_____

RIVAL 6

---◆---

MATERIALISM

"Seek God First"

Chapter Thirty-Six

Contentment Comes From God

Rival 6: Materialism

In a culture where success is measured by wealth, possessions, and status, materialism has become one of the most deceptive and destructive forces affecting Christians today. It promises happiness, security, and significance—but in reality, it silently undermines spiritual growth, weakens our relationship with God, and shifts our focus from the eternal to the temporary.

Materialism is more than just owning things—it's when things begin to own us. It is the excessive desire for wealth and possessions, the belief that having more will make us more, and the constant striving for what's next, newer, or better. While Scripture doesn't condemn wealth itself, it clearly warns us about the danger of making it our pursuit, our identity, or our god.

Let's explore how materialism damages the Christian life and how we can protect our hearts from its influence.

1. Materialism Shifts Our Focus from God to Self

At its core, materialism places self at the center. It drives us to chase comfort, appearance, and financial gain more than God's will. Jesus made it clear: "No one can serve two masters... You cannot serve both God and money" (Matthew 6:24).

When Christians fall into materialism, their priorities subtly shift. Time with God gets replaced with time pursuing income. Obedience to God's calling takes a back seat to career advancement. Contentment fades, and comparison sets in.

Instead of seeking first the Kingdom of God (Matthew 6:33), materialism causes believers to seek first the things of this world—even if they appear harmless or justifiable.

2. Materialism Breeds Discontentment

Materialism thrives on the lie that what you have is never enough. It fosters a constant sense of dissatisfaction and the fear of missing out. You begin to measure yourself by what you own or don't own, comparing your life to others on social media, in your church, or at your workplace.

Paul writes in Philippians 4:11–12 that he had "learned to be content whatever the circumstances." Contentment is learned through trusting in Christ, not in accumulating stuff. Materialism robs Christians of joy and peace by making them feel like they always need more to be happy, secure, or successful.

3. Materialism Chokes Spiritual Growth

In the Parable of the Sower (Mark 4:19), Jesus describes seeds (God's Word) falling among thorns. He says,
"But the worries of this life, the deceitfulness of wealth, and the desires for other things come in and choke the word, making it unfruitful."

This is a perfect picture of how materialism operates. It distracts, deceives, and drowns out spiritual fruit. It makes it harder to hear God, serve others, or live generously. Even well-intentioned Christians can have their spiritual growth stifled because their energy is consumed by the pursuit of more.

4. Materialism Diminishes Generosity

Generosity is at the heart of the Gospel. God gave His only Son. Jesus gave His life. We are called to give our time, talents, and resources to bless others and advance the Kingdom.

But materialism says, *"Keep it for yourself. You earned it. You deserve it."* It tightens our grip and makes us fearful to give, worried that we won't have enough for ourselves.

Proverbs 11:24 says, "One person gives freely, yet gains even more; another withholds unduly, but comes to poverty." A generous heart reflects trust in

God as the Provider. A materialistic heart reflects trust in possessions as the provider.

5. Materialism Erodes Faith and Increases Anxiety

When our hope is in money or material things, we will always be on edge—worried about losing what we have or not having enough. This is why Jesus said, "Do not store up for yourselves treasures on earth... but store up treasures in heaven" (Matthew 6:19–20).

Materialism anchors our hearts to earthly things, and when those things are shaken, our faith is shaken, too. But faith built on Christ is stable, unshakable, and eternal.

How to Guard Your Heart Against Materialism

1. Practice Gratitude
   Regularly thank God for what you already have. Gratitude cultivates contentment and destroys envy.

2. Live Simply
   Choose to limit your wants. Learn to say, "I don't need more to be fulfilled."

3. Give Generously
   Make generosity a lifestyle. The more you give, the less power money has over you.

4. Focus on Eternal Things
   Invest in things that matter forever—your relationship with God, loving others, and advancing the Gospel.

5. Stay in the Word
   Let Scripture shape your values, not culture. The more time you spend in God's truth, the clearer you'll see what really matters.

Final Thoughts

Materialism is subtle, seductive, and spiritually dangerous. It promises happiness but delivers emptiness. It masquerades as ambition but leads to anxiety. As Christians, we must constantly check our hearts and priorities, asking, "Am I living for eternity, or am I chasing the temporary?" God doesn't condemn wealth—but He does call us to steward it wisely, hold it loosely, and never worship it. The more we fix our eyes on Jesus, the less appealing the empty promises of materialism become. Choose contentment over consumption. Choose eternal treasures over earthly ones. And above all, choose God over everything else.

Taking Action

Think | Write | Grow

Based on what you learned in this chapter:

What's something you will stop doing or a habit you will break?

_____

_____

What's something you will start doing or a habit you will create?

_____

_____

What's the potential positive impact of improving in this area?

_____

_____

Chapter Thirty-Seven

Your Heart and Treasure Are Joined

Rival 6: Materialism

In Matthew 6:21, Jesus said, *"For where your treasure is, there your heart will be also."* With this simple but profound statement, He revealed a spiritual principle that still challenges and convicts us today. What we treasure—what we value, pursue, and prioritize—will always shape the direction and focus of our hearts.

In a world that constantly promotes success through possessions, status, and wealth, materialism has become one of the greatest competitors for our hearts. It promises happiness, identity, and security—but subtly pulls us away from the deeper relationship Christ wants to have with us.

So, what did Jesus mean by "where your treasure is," and how does materialism damage our walk with Him?

Where Is Your Treasure?

In the verses surrounding Matthew 6:21, Jesus warns His followers not to store up treasures on earth—things that can rust, rot, or be stolen. Instead, He encourages them to invest in eternal things: God's Kingdom, people's souls, and righteous living.

Treasure, in this context, refers not only to our money or possessions, but to whatever we deeply value and pursue. It's what fills our thoughts, fuels our decisions, and consumes our energy. Jesus' message is clear: what you treasure reveals what you truly love—and whom you ultimately serve.

If our treasure is in earthly gain, our hearts will be anchored in this temporary world. But if our treasure is in Christ and His Kingdom, our hearts will be anchored in eternity.

How Materialism Creeps In

Materialism isn't just about owning things—it's when things begin to own us. It's a subtle shift from enjoying blessings to idolizing them. It's found in the desire to always have more, the fear of not having enough, or the belief that our worth is tied to what we own.

In today's culture, materialism often disguises itself as ambition, success, or self-care. We're encouraged to accumulate, upgrade, and chase the next best thing. But over time, this pursuit becomes a spiritual distraction—pulling our focus from Christ to comfort, from generosity to greed, and from contentment to comparison.

Jesus warned in Matthew 6:24, *"You cannot serve both God and money."* That's because materialism doesn't just distract—it divides the heart. And a divided heart cannot fully love or follow Christ.

The Spiritual Consequences of Materialism

1. It Shifts Our Trust Away from God
   When we put our hope in wealth or possessions, we stop relying on God as our provider. We begin to trust in what we can see and control instead of the One who holds all things. Proverbs 11:28 says, *"Those who trust in their riches will fall."*

2. It Stifles Generosity
   Materialism makes it hard to give freely because it convinces us we never have "enough." But Christ calls us to be stewards, not hoarders. He blesses us so we can bless others—not just to increase our comfort.

3. It Numbs Us to Eternal Purpose
   When our lives revolve around accumulation, we lose sight of eternity. We stop asking, "How can I serve God's Kingdom?" and start asking, "What can I get for myself?" Jesus said in Luke 12:15, *"Life does not consist in an abundance of possessions."*

4. It Distances Us From Christ
The more we chase earthly treasures, the less we hunger for spiritual ones. Over time, materialism can dull our love for Jesus, weaken our prayer life, and make our faith shallow and performance-based.

How to Redirect Our Treasure—and Our Heart

1. Reexamine Your Priorities
Ask yourself regularly: *What am I truly living for? Where does most of my time, money, and energy go?* If your answers consistently point to earthly things, it may be time to realign your heart with God's priorities.

2. Practice Simplicity and Contentment
Learn to live with less and enjoy more of God. 1 Timothy 6:6 says, *"Godliness with contentment is great gain."* Contentment isn't settling—it's seeing God as enough.

3. Give Generously and Joyfully
Generosity is one of the fastest ways to break materialism's grip. When you give to others, to your church, and to missions, you remind your heart that your treasure is in God's Kingdom, not in this world.

4. Fix Your Eyes on Jesus
Hebrews 12:2 calls us to *"fix our eyes on Jesus, the author and perfecter of our faith."* The more we focus on Christ—His love, His mission, His promises—the less we are seduced by the temporary things of this world.

Final Thoughts

Jesus didn't say, *"Where your heart is, there your treasure will be."* He said the opposite: *"Where your treasure is, there your heart will be also."* That means you have the power to choose what shapes your heart—by choosing where to invest your time, attention, and resources. Materialism may be a powerful force in this world, but it is no match for the joy and peace that come from loving and serving Christ above all. When your treasure is in Him, your heart will follow—and you'll find a life of deeper meaning, greater freedom, and eternal reward. So, ask yourself, what do I treasure most? Because that is where my heart will live.

Taking Action

Think | Write | Grow

Based on what you learned in this chapter:

What's something you will stop doing or a habit you will break?

_____

_____

What's something you will start doing or a habit you will create?

_____

_____

What's the potential positive impact of improving in this area?

_____

_____

Chapter Thirty-Eight

Our Battle Is as Old as Time

Rival 6: Materialism

Throughout the Old Testament, no enemy challenged Israel as consistently and aggressively as the Philistines. They weren't just a military threat—they were a persistent spiritual rival that opposed the values, purpose, and calling of God's people. Beyond their historical role, the Philistines represented something far more dangerous—they symbolized the flesh, materialism, and worldly opposition to God's ways. Their influence didn't just test Israel's strength in battle—it tested Israel's faith, identity, and obedience.

The Philistines appeared throughout key moments in Israel's history, from the days of Samson and Samuel to the reigns of Saul and David. Again and again, they surfaced to disrupt God's plans and tempt Israel away from faithfulness. For modern believers, their story offers a powerful picture of the battle we all face—the struggle between living by the Spirit or giving in to the flesh and the pull of materialism.

1. The Philistines Opposed God's People at Every Turn

The Philistines were not a one-time threat. They repeatedly attacked and oppressed Israel, even occupying territory that God had promised to His people. This ongoing conflict made them more than enemies—they were a constant obstacle, always trying to drive Israel back to a place of defeat.

This reflects how the flesh works in the life of a believer. The flesh doesn't go away quietly. It continues to resist the Spirit, to challenge spiritual growth, and to reclaim ground that belongs to God. Like the Philistines, our carnal desires and worldly attachments show up again and again, trying to pull us away from what God has promised us.

2. They Represented Idolatry and False Worship

The Philistines were idol worshippers. Their primary god, Dagon, was a symbol of fertility and grain. They relied on pagan rituals, immoral practices, and demonic influences. Their spiritual values were directly opposed to the holiness of the God of Israel.

This opposition symbolizes the battle between true worship and the idolatry of the flesh. Today's version of Dagon may not be a carved statue, but the obsession with money, success, power, and sensual pleasure plays a similar role. The Philistines remind us that when we flirt with worldly values, we risk falling into spiritual compromise.

3. They Dominated Through Power, Wealth, and Control

The Philistines were technologically advanced and economically strong. In 1 Samuel 13, they had such control over the iron industry that the Israelites were forced to go to them just to sharpen their tools. Their dominance came not only from weapons but from economic manipulation.

This paints a clear picture of how materialism works. The love of money and power often holds people captive. Materialism promises security, but delivers bondage. It controls rather than frees. Just as Israel was weakened under the Philistine economy, believers today can be spiritually weakened when possessions become the center of life. When our trust shifts from God to material things, the flesh wins.

4. They Lured Israel Into Moral Compromise

The story of Samson is one of the most powerful examples of how the Philistines led God's people into moral downfall. Samson, a judge of Israel with incredible strength and divine purpose, was continually drawn to Philistine women. His relationship with Delilah led to betrayal, capture, and personal ruin.

This isn't just a story about lust—it's a story about how compromise begins. The Philistines represent the seductive nature of the flesh. What starts as curiosity or attraction can lead to spiritual blindness and defeat. Samson lost more than his strength—he lost sight of his calling. When believers entertain the flesh, they slowly surrender their spiritual authority.

5. They Blinded and Humiliated God's Servant

When the Philistines captured Samson, they gouged out his eyes, chained him, and used him as entertainment. This wasn't just a punishment—it was symbolic. Samson lost his physical sight, but it represented his earlier spiritual blindness. The enemy rejoiced while a once-powerful man of God was reduced to a spectacle.

This is what unchecked flesh and materialism does. They blind us, bind us, and rob us of dignity and spiritual power. The Philistines were more than captors—they were a picture of what happens when the people of God trade holiness for pleasure and mission for self-indulgence.

6. They Required Faith to Defeat

When Goliath, the Philistine giant, challenged Israel, the army was paralyzed by fear. Only David, a young shepherd, had the courage to stand against him—not with armor, but with faith in God. David's victory over Goliath wasn't just a military win—it was a spiritual breakthrough.

The only way to defeat the flesh and materialism is through faith, obedience, and total dependence on God. Human strength won't win this battle. It takes a heart fully surrendered to God's authority and a refusal to bow to fear or cultural pressure.

Final Thoughts

The Philistines were Israel's greatest earthly rival, but they also represent the greatest spiritual rivals we face today—flesh, sin, and the worship of material things. They opposed everything God wanted to build in His people. They attacked, tempted, enslaved, and corrupted. Yet, with every conflict, God raised up deliverers to remind Israel—and us—that victory is possible when we walk in the Spirit and place our treasure in God, not in the world. The battle with the "Philistines" of our soul is not just about resisting temptation. It's about remembering who we are, who we serve, and what matters most. Christ didn't just call us to escape defeat—He called us to live in victory. And that means, every day, we choose to serve the Spirit over the flesh, and eternal treasure over temporary gain.

Taking Action

Think | Write | Grow

Based on what you learned in this chapter:

What's something you will stop doing or a habit you will break?

_____

_____

What's something you will start doing or a habit you will create?

_____

_____

What's the potential positive impact of improving in this area?

_____

_____

Chapter Thirty-Nine

Worldly Temptations Run Deep

Rival 6: Materialism

Throughout the Bible, we find story after story of men who were tempted by the world's influence—through power, wealth, pleasure, or the pressure to compromise. These stories aren't just ancient tales—they're timeless warnings and lessons for every believer facing the pull of the world today. God never hides the flaws of His people—instead, He reveals them to teach us how to live wisely, walk in humility, and cling to Him when the world tries to pull us away.

Here are some of the most powerful and popular Bible stories where men were tempted by the world—and what we can learn from their victories or failures.

1. Adam (Genesis 3)

The first man in Scripture was also the first to fall to temptation. Adam, alongside Eve, was placed in a perfect garden with everything he needed. But when the serpent tempted Eve with the fruit from the tree of the knowledge of good and evil—promising that they would be "like God"—Adam gave in.

This wasn't just a temptation about fruit. It was a desire for power, independence, and self-exaltation—the very things the world still promises today. Adam's fall introduced sin into the world and separated humanity from God, proving that surrendering to worldly desires leads to destruction.

Lesson: Temptation often appears as something good, but leads to bondage. Disobedience to God always has a cost.

2. Lot (Genesis 13, 19)

Lot, Abraham's nephew, chose to settle near the city of Sodom because it was rich and fertile. But over time, he moved deeper into the city, eventually living among a culture that was corrupt and godless. Though Lot was considered righteous, his choice to live close to sin weakened his witness, cost him his home, and brought devastation to his family.

Lot's story shows how the comfort, wealth, and convenience of the world can slowly draw us into compromise. He chose based on what looked appealing—not what was spiritually safe.

Lesson: Don't pitch your tent near compromise. The more you entertain the world's values, the more you risk losing what matters most.

3. Samson (Judges 13–16)

Samson was a man anointed by God with supernatural strength to deliver Israel from the Philistines. But he had a weakness for women, particularly those from enemy nations. His involvement with Delilah, who seduced him and discovered the secret of his strength, led to his capture, blindness, and humiliation.

Samson was called to lead, but he let lust and pleasure lead him. Though God eventually restored his strength, his story is a sobering reminder of how worldly temptation can derail even the most gifted people.

Lesson: God's gifts do not exempt you from temptation. Yielding to the flesh always leads to loss unless repented of.

4. King Saul (1 Samuel 15)

Saul started out as a humble man but quickly gave in to the fear of man and the pressure to please people. In 1 Samuel 15, he disobeyed God by sparing King Agag and the best of the Amalekite possessions instead of destroying everything as God had commanded.

When confronted by the prophet Samuel, Saul confessed that he feared the people and gave in to their wishes. His compromise cost him the kingdom.

Lesson: When we seek the world's approval over God's commands, we lose more than influence—we lose God's favor and purpose for our lives.

5. King Solomon (1 Kings 11)

Solomon was the wisest man who ever lived, but even he wasn't immune to temptation. Despite building the temple and writing books of wisdom, Solomon allowed his many foreign wives to turn his heart toward other gods. He compromised his faith for political alliances, pleasure, and luxury.

Solomon's heart was divided, and his legacy was tarnished by idolatry and disobedience.

Lesson: Success and wisdom are not enough if your heart isn't fully devoted to God. The world offers many distractions, but only God deserves your full loyalty.

Final Thoughts

From Adam to Demas, the Bible is filled with real stories of men who were tempted by the world's influence—some who overcame, and others who fell. The common thread is clear: the world's promises are always temporary, but God's truth is eternal. These stories are not just cautionary tales—they are wake-up calls. They challenge us to examine our own hearts, stay alert to temptation, and lean on the Word of God for strength. In a world that pulls hard in every direction, only those rooted in Christ can stand firm. Let these stories remind you: the world may tempt, but only God truly satisfies.

Taking Action

Think | Write | Grow

Based on what you learned in this chapter:

What's something you will stop doing or a habit you will break?

_____

_____

What's something you will start doing or a habit you will create?

_____

_____

What's the potential positive impact of improving in this area?

_____

_____

Chapter Forty

Greed Is Subtle and Dangerous

Rival 6: Materialism

G reed is one of the most subtle and spiritually dangerous sins a Christian can fall into. While it often disguises itself as ambition, financial wisdom, or personal success, greed is ultimately a misplaced hunger for more—more wealth, more status, more security, or more possessions—often at the cost of spiritual health, relationships, and contentment.

The Bible repeatedly warns us about the dangers of greed, not because God is against wealth or progress, but because greed shifts our trust away from Him and feeds a spirit of idolatry, pride, and discontent. It tempts believers to serve two masters and to value the temporary over the eternal.

What Is Greed?

Greed is an intense and selfish desire for something, especially wealth, power, or possessions. It is the constant craving for more—not for provision, but for accumulation and control. Greed isn't just about money. It can take the form of hoarding time, manipulating relationships for gain, or refusing to share what you have. It's a heart posture that says, *"What I have is never enough, and I deserve more—even at others' expense."*

Jesus warned clearly about this mindset in Luke 12:15: "Watch out! Be on your guard against all kinds of greed; life does not consist in an abundance of possessions."

The Dangers of Greed for Christians

1. Greed Shifts Trust Away from God

At its core, greed is a sign of misplaced trust. Rather than depending on God as Provider, the greedy heart relies on money, possessions, or success to feel secure. This is why Paul says in 1 Timothy 6:10: "For the love of money is a root of all kinds of evil." It's not money itself that is evil—it's the love of it, the obsession with it, the belief that it can meet our deepest needs.

When Christians give in to greed, they stop seeking first the Kingdom of God and start seeking first their own gain.

2. Greed Leads to Idolatry

Colossians 3:5 says, "Put to death... greed, which is idolatry." Why idolatry? Because greed puts something else—money, success, or possessions—in the place that only God should occupy.

It says, *"If I have this, I'll be happy. If I achieve this, I'll be secure."* It replaces faith with materialism and worship with self-interest.

3. Greed Erodes Contentment and Gratitude

A greedy heart is never satisfied. It constantly compares, envies, and strives for more—leaving little room for peace, thankfulness, or joy.

Paul wrote in Philippians 4:11–12, "I have learned the secret of being content... whether well fed or hungry, whether living in plenty or in want." That secret was found in Christ—not in accumulation.

Greed steals contentment by keeping our eyes on what we lack instead of what God has already provided.

4. Greed Damages Relationships and Community

Greed can make people manipulative, selfish, and even dishonest. It drives people to use others rather than serve them. It undermines trust, breeds division, and weakens generosity.

Acts 2:44–45 shows the early Church living in radical generosity and unity. Greed does the opposite—it isolates and divides by convincing us that we must protect "what's ours" rather than bless others with it.

What Is the Root of Greed?

The root of greed is not financial need—it's fear, pride, and unbelief.

- Fear that there won't be enough

- Pride that believes we deserve more

- Unbelief that doubts God's ability to provide

Greed ultimately reveals a heart that does not trust God to take care of us. It says, *"God might not come through, so I need to take control."* This is the same lie Satan used in the Garden of Eden, whispering to Eve that what God provided wasn't enough.

How to Guard Against Greed

1. Practice Generosity
Greed hoards. Generosity frees. Giving to others—especially when it costs us—breaks greed's grip and teaches us to trust God more than our money.

2. Cultivate Gratitude
Thank God daily for what you already have. Gratitude refocuses your heart from "I need more" to "God has already given me enough."

3. Renew Your Mind with Scripture
Fill your thoughts with God's truth about provision, contentment, and an eternal perspective. Let His Word shape your values, not the world's promises.

4. Remember the Eternal
Matthew 6:19–20 reminds us, "Do not store up for yourselves treasures on earth... but store up for yourselves treasures in heaven." Greed lives for now. Faith lives for eternity.

Final Thoughts

Greed is more than just wanting more—it's a heart condition that competes with God for your trust, worship, and affection. It destroys peace, erodes contentment, and deceives even sincere believers into believing that abundance comes from wealth, not from Christ. But Jesus offers something better: freedom from fear, fullness of joy, and the peace of knowing that He is enough. The cure to greed is not more stuff—it's more trust. The more we trust God as our Provider, the less we need to cling to the things of this world. Choose generosity over greed, faith over fear, and eternal treasure over temporary gain—and you will find that God is always more than enough.

Taking Action

Think | Write | Grow

Based on what you learned in this chapter:

What's something you will stop doing or a habit you will break?

_____

_____

What's something you will start doing or a habit you will create?

_____

_____

What's the potential positive impact of improving in this area?

_____

_____

Chapter Forty-One

Sowing to Reap Is God's Way

Rival 6: Materialism

I n the world of faith and finances, the terms "giving to get" and "sowing to reap" often get used interchangeably—but they reflect two very different heart postures and spiritual principles. While both involve giving, only one aligns with the selfless, faith-filled model taught in Scripture.

One is transactional and self-focused—giving only to receive. The other is biblical and transformational—planting seeds in faith, knowing that God brings increase in His way and timing. Understanding the difference is essential for any Christian who wants to live a life of generosity that honors God and reflects His Kingdom principles.

Giving to Get: The World's Twist on a Kingdom Concept

"Giving to get" is the mindset that treats generosity like a business deal with God: *"If I give this, I expect something in return."* It may sound spiritual on the surface, but it's rooted in greed, manipulation, and self-interest. This mentality reduces giving to a formula—invest X amount and expect Y return, usually in the form of wealth, blessings, or success.

This kind of giving is often promoted in prosperity teachings, where the focus shifts from honoring God to using God. It turns generosity into a tool for personal gain, rather than an act of worship, obedience, and trust.

Jesus warned against this mindset in Matthew 6:1–4, where He told His followers not to give with the motive of being noticed or rewarded by people. He emphasized that giving should be done in secret, with humility, and for the glory of God—not for personal payoff.

Sowing to Reap: A Biblical Principle of Faith and Trust

"Sowing to reap," on the other hand, is a God-ordained principle that reflects His design for creation, stewardship, and blessing. It is rooted in Galatians 6:7: "Do not be deceived: God cannot be mocked. A man reaps what he sows."

This law of sowing and reaping applies to all areas of life—not just finances. When we sow seeds of kindness, love, truth, time, and resources, we position ourselves to reap a harvest in due season. But the difference lies in the motivation.

Sowing is:

- Faithful, not forceful

- Worship, not manipulation

- Purposeful, not selfish

2 Corinthians 9:6–7 echoes this:
"Whoever sows sparingly will also reap sparingly, and whoever sows generously will also reap generously. Each one should give what he has decided in his heart, not reluctantly or under compulsion, for God loves a cheerful giver."

This kind of giving comes from a heart of gratitude, trust, and obedience. It acknowledges that everything we have belongs to God, and we are simply stewards sowing into His purposes.

Why Sowing to Reap Is a Godly Law

Sowing and reaping is a spiritual law established by God, just as real as the law of gravity. From Genesis to Revelation, we see this principle at work:

- Genesis 8:22—"As long as the earth endures... seedtime and harvest... will never cease."

- Proverbs 11:24–25—"One gives freely, yet grows all the richer... whoever brings blessing will be enriched."

- Luke 6:38—"Give, and it will be given to you... For with the measure you use, it will be measured back to you."

God honors sowing because it reflects His heart—He is a giver. When we give with the intent to bless others and advance His Kingdom, we align with His nature and open the door to supernatural fruitfulness.

But unlike "giving to get," sowing is not transactional—it's transformational. We don't give to force God's hand, but to express faith that He is faithful. The harvest may not always be financial—it might be peace, relationships, spiritual growth, or open doors we never expected.

How to Sow in a God-Honoring Way

1. Examine Your Motives
   Ask: *Am I giving to manipulate God, or to honor Him?*

2. Give Cheerfully and Generously
   God delights in a heart that gives with joy, not reluctance.

3. Trust God with the Harvest
   Leave the outcome to Him. Your job is to plant faithfully.

4. Sow in All Areas of Life
   Don't limit sowing to money. Sow encouragement, service, love, and truth.

5. Be Patient and Persistent
   Galatians 6:9 reminds us: "Let us not grow weary in doing good, for in due season we will reap, if we do not give up."

Final Thoughts

"Giving to get" is short-sighted and self-centered. "Sowing to reap" is biblical, wise, and God-glorifying. It is an act of faith, not a formula for prosperity. When we sow with the right heart—trusting God, honoring His Word, and blessing others—we align ourselves with the unshakable law of God's Kingdom. So don't give just to receive. Sow generously, trust deeply, and expect a harvest—not because you deserve it, but because God is faithful.

Taking Action

Think | Write | Grow

B ased on what you learned in this chapter:

What's something you will stop doing or a habit you will break?

_____

_____

What's something you will start doing or a habit you will create?

_____

_____

What's the potential positive impact of improving in this area?

_____

_____

Chapter Forty-Two

Materialism Is Rooted in Fear

Rival 6: Materialism

In a world driven by consumerism, image, and the endless pursuit of "more," materialism has become one of the greatest spiritual threats to modern Christians. It's subtle, seductive, and socially accepted. But beneath the polished surface of accumulating things lies a deeper problem—fear. Fear of not having enough. Fear of falling behind. Fear of being unseen or unloved. Materialism doesn't just grow from desire—it grows from distrust—a lack of trust in God's provision, identity, and purpose.

But there is a solution, and it's not found in minimalism, budgeting apps, or financial discipline alone. It's found in trusting God. When we place our confidence in Him and refuse to let fear rule our decisions, materialism loses its grip.

Materialism Is Rooted in Fear and Insecurity

At its core, materialism is a response to internal fear—fear that we won't be secure without money, won't be valued without the right status symbols, or won't be happy without more. The constant craving for more clothes, nicer cars, better devices, or bigger titles often masks a deep spiritual restlessness.

Jesus addressed this directly in Matthew 6:25-32 when He said not to worry about food, drink, or clothing. He pointed out how God cares for the birds and clothes the flowers—and reminded us how much more valuable we are. Fear drives worry, worry fuels materialism, and trust cancels both.

Trusting God Breaks the Cycle of Fear

When we truly trust God, we believe:

- He knows what we need before we ask.

- He is our provider—not our job, salary, or savings account.

- He gives us identity, value, and security apart from material things.

Trusting God means we don't chase after what the world chases. We stop trying to keep up appearances or build our worth through possessions. We stop using things to fill the gaps only God can fill.

Proverbs 3:5-6 reminds us to "trust in the Lord with all your heart and lean not on your own understanding." This isn't passive belief—it's active surrender. It means we stop trusting in wealth, image, or worldly comfort and start building our lives on the promises of God.

Trust Produces Contentment, Not Comparison

Materialism thrives in a culture of comparison. When we fear not being "enough," we try to compensate with things that make us feel superior or secure. But trust in God births contentment—a rare and powerful antidote.

Paul wrote in Philippians 4:11-13 that he had learned to be content in all circumstances—whether in plenty or in want. Why? Because his strength and satisfaction came from Christ, not his possessions.

When we trust God, we stop asking, "What do I lack?" and begin declaring, "God is enough." That contentment silences the voice of fear and the noise of materialism.

Trust Frees Us to Be Generous

One of the surest signs we trust God is that we become more generous. Materialism clutches. Trust releases. Fear hoards. Faith gives. When we trust God as our source, we don't panic when we give. We don't view generosity as loss, but as worship. We recognize that all we have is from Him, and we're simply stewards of His blessings.

2 Corinthians 9:6-8 reminds us that God loves a cheerful giver and is able to bless us abundantly so that we always have what we need. Trusting this promise allows us to live open-handedly and joyfully, defeating the grip of greed and the illusion of ownership.

Fear Is a Liar—Trust Tells the Truth

Fear whispers, "You're not enough. You need more. You won't make it." But trust declares, "God is my provider. He sees me. He knows my needs. He won't fail." The more we trust in God's character and promises, the less influence fear has over our decisions. As fear fades, materialism weakens, and our hearts grow rich in faith, love, and purpose.

Final Thoughts

Materialism is not just a money issue—it's a trust issue. It's the fruit of fear trying to find safety and identity in things. But when we trust God, fear loses its voice. We no longer live for possessions, but for His purpose. We find contentment in His presence, not in purchases. We give generously because we believe He will provide. The cure for materialism isn't found in guilt or restraint—it's found in faith. When we trust God completely and refuse to live in fear, we declare that He is enough—and in that declaration, materialism dies.

Taking Action

Think | Write | Grow

Based on what you learned in this chapter:

What's something you will stop doing or a habit you will break?

_____

_____

What's something you will start doing or a habit you will create?

_____

_____

What's the potential positive impact of improving in this area?

_____

_____

RIVAL 7

WORLD INFLUENCE

"Walk the Narrow Path"

Chapter Forty-Three

Satan Was Created and Is Limited

Rival 7: World Influence

There is a common misconception in the world—and even among some Christians—that Satan is God's equal opposite. Many imagine a cosmic war between two equally powerful forces: God, representing good, and Satan, representing evil. This idea is not only unbiblical, but it is dangerous. It gives Satan too much credit and diminishes the glory and sovereignty of God. The truth is simple and clear: Satan is a created being. He is not equal to God, he is not eternal, and he is not all-powerful.

To understand Satan's true position, we have to start at the beginning. Satan, often referred to by his former name Lucifer, was originally created by God as a beautiful and powerful angel. He was not evil when he was made. Scripture suggests he held a high-ranking position among the angels and was full of wisdom and beauty. But pride entered his heart, and he rebelled against God, seeking to exalt himself above his Creator. This rebellion caused him to fall from his heavenly position.

The fact that Satan was created means he is not self-existent. Unlike God, who has no beginning and no end, Satan had a starting point. He owes his very existence to the Creator he rebelled against. That alone proves he is not God's equal. God is infinite, eternal, and sovereign. Satan is finite, temporal, and subject to divine authority.

Not only is Satan a created being, but he is also severely limited in power. He is not all-knowing, all-present, and all-powerful. These are attributes that belong to God alone. Satan cannot be in more than one place at a time. He cannot read minds or know the future with certainty. He must operate through deception, temptation, and manipulation because he lacks the power to force anything upon us without permission or influence.

Throughout the Bible, Satan is portrayed as having to ask God for permission to act in certain situations. In the story of Job, Satan had to receive God's approval before he could touch Job's life. This shows us clearly that Satan operates within boundaries set by God. He is not free to act as he pleases. Even his most malicious schemes are ultimately constrained by God's sovereign hand.

Many people also wrongly believe that Satan is eternal, like God. But Satan is not immortal in the sense of having existed forever or continuing forever in power. He will one day be permanently and publicly judged. The Bible is clear about his end—he will be cast into the lake of fire for eternal punishment. That means his influence has an expiration date. His authority is temporary. His reign of deception will come to a complete and final halt.

This truth should bring comfort and confidence to every believer. We are not caught in an endless battle between two gods. We serve the one true God, who has no rival and no equal. Satan's power is real, but it is limited. His existence is temporary. His defeat is certain. Jesus Christ, through His death and resurrection, has already disarmed and defeated Satan's authority. We are not fighting for victory—we are standing in the victory Christ has already won.

Knowing that Satan is a created and limited being should also help us resist fear. He is not in control. He is not unstoppable. His weapons—temptation, accusation, deception—are powerful only when we believe his lies. When we stand firm in the truth of God's Word and walk in the authority of Jesus, Satan has no foothold.

It is essential that we do not inflate Satan's role or power beyond what Scripture teaches. Doing so only breeds fear, confusion, and spiritual defeat. At the same time, we should not ignore his existence or dismiss his influence. The balanced, biblical view is this: Satan is real, he is dangerous, but he is defeated, created, limited, and subject to God's final judgment.

Final Thoughts

God has no equal, no rival, and no competition. He alone is Lord over all creation. Satan may rage for a season, but his fate is sealed. He is not the king of darkness—he is a fallen angel awaiting judgment. As believers, we have been given power through Christ to stand against his schemes and live in victory. In the end, the truth is clear and freeing: Satan is not equal to God. He is a created being, he is limited, and he is not eternal. And because of Jesus, we do not fight for victory—we fight from victory. Let that truth shape how you pray, how you walk, and how you live.

Taking Action

Think | Write | Grow

Based on what you learned in this chapter:

What's something you will stop doing or a habit you will break?

_____

_____

What's something you will start doing or a habit you will create?

_____

_____

What's the potential positive impact of improving in this area?

_____

_____

Chapter Forty-Four

Jesus Beat Satan With Scripture

Rival 7: World Influence

B efore Jesus began His public ministry, He was led by the Spirit into the wilderness to face a direct confrontation with Satan. For forty days, Jesus fasted and endured intense temptation. In Matthew 4:1–11, we see this powerful encounter unfold—not as a myth or metaphor, but as a real, spiritual battle. Jesus' time in the wilderness was not just a test of His strength—it was a vivid picture of the believer's struggle with worldly influence and a model for how to overcome it.

In every temptation Jesus faced, Satan appealed to worldly desires—physical needs, personal pride, and the hunger for power. These same influences still war against believers today. But through Jesus' example, we find hope and a clear strategy to resist and stand strong.

Let's examine how each of Satan's temptations reflects the world's influence on us—and how Jesus shows us the way to defeat it.

1. The Temptation of Physical Satisfaction

Satan's first challenge came when Jesus was at His weakest, physically. After 40 days without food, Satan said, "If you are the Son of God, command these stones to become bread" (Matthew 4:3). The enemy's appeal wasn't just about hunger—it was about using power to satisfy immediate, fleshly desires.

This reflects one of the world's loudest messages: *"If you want it, you deserve it—now."* Whether it's food, pleasure, or comfort, the world constantly tells us to indulge ourselves, even at the cost of obedience.

But Jesus replied, "Man shall not live by bread alone, but by every word that comes from the mouth of God" (Matthew 4:4). Instead of giving in to desire, He affirmed that God's Word and God's will are more satisfying and more important than temporary gratification.

Lesson: When faced with worldly urges, choose spiritual nourishment over quick relief. Trust that God's timing and provision are better than self-serving shortcuts.

2. The Temptation of Pride and Performance

Satan took Jesus to the top of the temple and challenged Him to jump, quoting Scripture to justify it. "If you are the Son of God," Satan said, "throw yourself down... He will command His angels to protect you" (Matthew 4:6).

Here, Satan tried to provoke pride and self-exaltation, urging Jesus to prove His identity through spectacle and performance. This mirrors how the world often pressures us to validate ourselves by what we do, how we appear, or how we're perceived.

Jesus answered, "It is written: 'You shall not put the Lord your God to the test'" (Matthew 4:7). He didn't need to prove Himself to anyone—not even Satan—because His identity was secure in the Father's love.

Lesson: Resist the world's demand for validation through performance. When your identity is rooted in God, you don't need to seek approval from the crowd.

3. The Temptation of Power and Possessions

Finally, Satan showed Jesus all the kingdoms of the world and said, "All this I will give you, if you bow down and worship me" (Matthew 4:9). This was a direct appeal to power, glory, and material wealth—offered at the price of compromise.

This temptation echoes the world's obsession with success, influence, and wealth. Satan essentially offered a shortcut to kingship without the cross. But Jesus answered, "Away from me, Satan! For it is written: Worship the Lord your God, and serve Him only." (Matthew 4:10).

Jesus made it clear that worship belongs to God alone, and no promise of worldly gain is worth betraying that truth.

Lesson: Don't sell your soul for temporary success. True victory is found in obedience to God, not in the riches or recognition the world offers.

How We Can Overcome Worldly Influence

Jesus didn't overcome Satan in the wilderness through debate, force, or compromise. He overcame by standing on the truth of God's Word and remaining fully committed to His Father's will.

As followers of Christ, we face the same tactics. The world constantly tempts us to prioritize comfort over calling, applause over obedience, and power over humility. But Jesus shows us a better way.

Here's how we can resist and overcome:

- Know the Word of God: Every response Jesus gave began with, "It is written." Truth is your greatest weapon against lies.

- Stay Spirit-led: Jesus was led into the wilderness by the Holy Spirit. We must walk closely with the Spirit to discern truth from deception.

- Recognize the enemy's voice: Satan often twists Scripture and disguises lies as good offers. Don't fall for the bait—test everything against God's Word.

- Keep your worship pure, because only God deserves your devotion. Don't let success, fame, or possessions take His place.

Final Thoughts

Jesus' wilderness experience wasn't just a personal trial—it was a public declaration that the Kingdom of God operates by a different standard than the world. He showed us that we can resist the world's influence, but only by depending on God, valuing His Word, and keeping our eyes on eternal things. In a world filled with noise, temptation, and distraction, Jesus' example stands as a clear call: worship God alone, stand on His truth, and trust that victory comes through obedience—not compromise. The wilderness may be hard, but with Christ, we can walk through it and come out stronger, purer, and closer to God.

Taking Action

Think | Write | Grow

Based on what you learned in this chapter:

What's something you will stop doing or a habit you will break?

_____

_____

What's something you will start doing or a habit you will create?

_____

_____

What's the potential positive impact of improving in this area?

_____

_____

Chapter Forty-Five

Be In the World, Not of the World

Rival 7: World Influence

W e live in a time where headlines are heavy, opinions are loud, and anxiety seems to be everywhere. Global conflict, economic uncertainty, political division, social unrest, moral decline—the list of reasons to worry grows longer every day. It's easy, even for Christians, to become overwhelmed by the chaos and feel consumed by fear, anger, or despair.them,

But the Bible gives us a different perspective: God is still on the throne, and His people are not called to panic, but to trust. Christians are not immune to the burdens of this world, but we are not supposed to be ruled by them, either. In fact, we are specifically instructed not to worry and not to get caught up in the world's drama and distress.

Here's why Christians shouldn't worry about everything happening around them—and how they can live with peace, focus, and purpose in uncertain times.

1. Worry Distracts Us From Trusting God

Jesus spoke directly to the issue of worry in Matthew 6:25–34. He told His followers three times: "Do not worry." He reminded them that God takes care of the birds and the flowers, and they are worth far more. He concluded by saying, *"Seek first the kingdom of God and His righteousness, and all these things will be added to you."*

Worry focuses our eyes on what might go wrong, while faith keeps our eyes fixed on the One who holds it all together. When we obsess over world events, we forget who's truly in control. God is not shaken. His promises are still true.

2. The World Is Not Our Home

Philippians 3:20 says, "But our citizenship is in heaven." As Christians, we are not called to fit in or be absorbed by the world. We are called to be in the world, but not of it (John 17:14–16). When we allow ourselves to get caught up in every news story, political debate, or cultural controversy, we risk forgetting that this world is temporary and our hope is eternal.

We should care about justice, truth, and righteousness. We should pray, vote, and stand up for what's right. But we should not be consumed by the fear, anger, or division that dominates the world. We live for a higher Kingdom with an unshakable King.

3. God Is Still Sovereign—Even When the World Looks Chaotic

Psalm 46 reminds us that God is our refuge and strength, a very present help in trouble. The psalm describes the earth shaking and nations raging, yet it declares that "the Lord Almighty is with us."

None of the events in today's world surprise God. He has seen empires rise and fall. He has worked through chaos before, and He will again. Nothing can stop His plans. While the world may be unstable, God's character is not. His goodness, justice, and sovereignty remain unchanged.

4. Worry Robs Us of Peace and Weakens Our Witness

When Christians live in fear, we lose our peace—and with it, our ability to reflect Christ to a fearful world. Philippians 4:6–7 tells us, "Do not be anxious about anything, but in every situation, by prayer and petition, with thanksgiving, present your requests to God. And the peace of God will guard your hearts and your minds in Christ Jesus."

We are called to be salt and light (Matthew 5:13–16). If we respond to the world's chaos the same way that the world does—with fear, outrage, or despair—we have nothing different to offer. But when we live with peace, hope, and steadiness, we show the world what faith looks like under pressure.

5. Jesus Has Already Overcome the World

In John 16:33, Jesus says, "In this world you will have trouble. But take heart! I have overcome the world."

Jesus never promised a life free from trials. He promised His presence in the middle of them. The good news is that no matter what happens in the world—whether it's economic collapse, political chaos, or cultural darkness—Jesus has already secured the victory.

Our job isn't to fix everything. Our job is to walk faithfully, love boldly, pray continually, and to trust fully. The rest is in God's hands.

How Christians Can Stay Grounded

1. Spend more time in God's Word than in the news.
   Let Scripture shape your outlook more than social media or headlines.

2. Pray more than you post.
   Turn your concerns into intercession. Bring every burden to God.

3. Focus on what you can control.
   Love your neighbor. Serve your community. Live out your faith where you are.

4. Encourage others with hope.
   Speak peace into fear. Remind others of God's promises.

Final Thoughts

Yes, the world is full of trouble—but it's also full of opportunities to shine God's light. Christians were never meant to live in fear or be swept away by cultural panic. We were meant to live differently—rooted in truth, grounded in peace, and anchored in Christ. So don't get caught up in everything that is going on around you. Keep your eyes on Jesus. Trust His Word. And remember that this world is not your home—and your hope is not in its systems. Your hope is in the One who never changes and whose Kingdom never ends.

Taking Action

Think | Write | Grow

Based on what you learned in this chapter:

What's something you will stop doing or a habit you will break?

_____

_____

What's something you will start doing or a habit you will create?

_____

_____

What's the potential positive impact of improving in this area?

_____

_____

Chapter Forty-Six

Balanced Is Better than Busy

Rival 7: World Influence

In today's fast-paced world, being busy has become a badge of honor. Calendars are packed, to-do lists are never-ending, and many Christians are caught in a whirlwind of responsibilities. While diligence and hard work are biblical values, constant busyness can actually distract us from what truly matters—our relationship with God, our families, and our spiritual peace.

In Luke 10:38–42, Jesus visits the home of Martha and Mary. While Mary sits at Jesus' feet, listening and drawing near to Him, Martha is distracted by all the tasks of hosting. Frustrated, she asks Jesus to tell Mary to help her. But Jesus gently responds:

"Martha, Martha, you are worried and upset about many things, but few things are needed—or indeed only one. Mary has chosen what is better, and it will not be taken away from her."

This moment reveals a powerful truth: It's possible to be so busy doing things for Jesus that we miss being with Jesus. And in that, we see the importance of work-life balance—not just for our mental and emotional well-being, but for our spiritual health as followers of Christ.

Martha's Busyness vs. Mary's Devotion

Martha wasn't doing anything wrong. She was serving, preparing, and likely trying to honor Jesus with her efforts. But her priorities were out of order. Her heart was anxious, distracted, and overwhelmed.

Mary, on the other hand, recognized that being present with Jesus mattered more than completing tasks. She didn't ignore responsibilities—she prioritized the eternal over the urgent. Jesus commended her, not for her inactivity, but for her focus and presence.

This story reminds us that balance is not about doing less—it's about choosing better.

Why Work-Life Balance Matters for Christians

1. Your Identity Is in Christ, Not in What You Do

Our culture often equates worth with productivity. But as believers, our value doesn't come from how much we get done—it comes from who we belong to. God doesn't love us more when we're busy or less when we rest. He desires relationship over performance.

Psalm 46:10 says, "Be still, and know that I am God." Stillness isn't laziness—it's trust and obedience. When we make space for God in our daily lives, we declare that He is in control, not us.

2. Constant Busyness Weakens Spiritual Focus

When life is unbalanced and overloaded, our spiritual disciplines suffer. Prayer becomes rushed. Scripture reading is skipped. Church becomes optional. The very things that fuel our faith get pushed aside for lesser things.

Jesus often withdrew from crowds to pray, even when demands were high (Luke 5:16). If the Son of God needed time to refocus and rest, how much more do we? Balance allows us to nourish our souls so that we can serve from a place of overflow, not exhaustion.

3. God Cares About Your Whole Life—Not Just Your Productivity

Some Christians believe that rest is selfish or that slowing down is unspiritual. But rest is biblical. God Himself rested after creation and instituted the Sabbath not as a burden, but as a gift for restoration (Exodus 20:8–11).

Balancing work, family, church, and rest honors God because it reflects healthy stewardship of the life He gave us. When we care for our bodies, our relationships, and our spiritual well-being, we honor Him more than when we run ourselves into the ground.

4. Balance Helps Us Love Others Better

When we're constantly busy like Martha, our hearts grow anxious, impatient, and resentful. We begin to serve out of obligation rather than love. But when we live with balance and spiritual clarity, we serve others with joy, energy, and genuine compassion.

Busyness without balance robs us of our ability to listen, connect, and be fully present with the people around us—just as Martha missed out on enjoying Jesus' presence because she was so consumed with tasks.

How to Live With Balance Instead of Burnout

1. Start With God Daily
   Even 10 minutes of prayer or Scripture reading can shift your mindset from chaos to calm. Begin each day by sitting at Jesus' feet.

2. Set Boundaries
   Learn to say no to good things in order to say yes to the best things. You don't have to be everything to everyone.

3. Honor the Sabbath
   Take one day a week to rest, reflect, and enjoy God's presence. Use it to recharge spiritually, physically, and emotionally.

4. Pursue Presence Over Productivity
   Choose moments of connection—whether with God, family, or friends—over constant doing. Life is richer when we slow down.

5. Let Go of Guilt
   Refuse to believe the lie that rest is laziness. Trust that God is pleased with you, even when you are resting.

Final Thoughts

Being like Martha may win the approval of people, but being like Mary wins the approval of Jesus. Work has its place. Serving others is important. But without balance, our efforts become noise rather than worship. Jesus didn't come to burden us with busyness—He came to give us life, and life more abundantly (John 10:10). That abundant life begins when we slow down, sit at His feet, and learn to live from a place of peace, purpose, and presence. Choose what's better. Let the world chase busyness. You, as a child of God, were made for balance—and for deeper fellowship with the One who calls you to rest.

Taking Action

Think | Write | Grow

Based on what you learned in this chapter:

What's something you will stop doing or a habit you will break?

_____

_____

What's something you will start doing or a habit you will create?

_____

_____

What's the potential positive impact of improving in this area?

_____

_____

Chapter Forty-Seven

Proverbs Is Advice From God

Rival 7: World Influence

I n a world full of noise, distractions, and shifting values, the Book of Proverbs stands as a timeless source of wisdom and direction. Written primarily by King Solomon, the wisest man to ever live, Proverbs is not just a collection of clever sayings—it is God-inspired truth designed to help us navigate life with discernment, integrity, and spiritual maturity.

Proverbs is deeply practical, addressing the very issues we face today: temptation, pride, laziness, greed, gossip, relationships, and the lure of worldly success. It is a book that doesn't just inform the mind—it transforms the heart, helping us resist the subtle pull of culture and stay rooted in God's truth.

Let's explore why the Book of Proverbs is so important for Christians today and how it equips us to avoid the traps of conforming to the world's influence.

Proverbs: God's Guide to Wisdom in Everyday Life

The core message of Proverbs is summed up in Proverbs 1:7: "The fear of the Lord is the beginning of knowledge, but fools despise wisdom and instruction." This verse establishes that true wisdom starts with reverence for God. It's not just about intelligence or cleverness—wisdom is living in right relationship with God and applying His truth to every area of life.

Proverbs teaches us how to think, speak, work, handle money, build relationships, and make decisions in ways that honor God and protect us from destruction. In a world that rewards shortcuts, celebrates rebellion, and redefines morality, Proverbs calls us back to the unchanging principles of godly living.

How Proverbs Helps Us Resist Conforming to the World

1. It Teaches Us to Recognize and Reject Foolishness

Throughout Proverbs, there is a clear contrast between the wise and the foolish. The fool is impulsive, arrogant, and blind to consequences. The world encourages us to live for the moment, follow our hearts, and define truth for ourselves—these are all marks of foolishness.

Proverbs 14:12 warns, "There is a way that seems right to a man, but its end is the way to death." This reminds us that just because something feels right or is popular doesn't mean it aligns with God's will. Proverbs helps us pause, evaluate, and choose the path of wisdom rather than conforming to destructive patterns.

2. It Guards Us Against the Power of Temptation

Proverbs dedicates many verses to warning against sexual immorality, greed, and flattery—all tactics the world uses to lure people into sin. The seductive voice of the world often promises freedom but delivers bondage.

Proverbs 7, for example, describes a young man being enticed by a seductive woman—a symbol of temptation. The chapter ends with a sobering truth: "Her house is a highway to the grave, leading down to the chambers of death." (Proverbs 7:27)

Proverbs helps us see beyond the bait to the trap. It trains our minds and hearts to value purity, self-control, and long-term consequences over short-term pleasure.

3. It Promotes Humility Over Pride

Pride is at the heart of much of the world's influence—it tells us to put ourselves first, elevate our opinions, and ignore correction. But Proverbs says, "Pride goes before destruction, and a haughty spirit before a fall." (Proverbs 16:18)

In contrast, Proverbs teaches that humility brings wisdom, favor, and honor. The world may celebrate arrogance and self-promotion, but God honors the humble. Proverbs reminds us that humility is the posture of the wise.

4. It Prioritizes Character Over Image

Today's culture values appearance, success, and popularity. But Proverbs focuses on what really matters: the condition of the heart.

- Proverbs 22:1—"A good name is more desirable than great riches."

- Proverbs 4:23—"Above all else, guard your heart, for everything you do flows from it."

Rather than chasing approval from the world, Proverbs teaches us to cultivate integrity, honesty, and righteousness—qualities that reflect God's character and set us apart from the world's standards.

5. It Calls Us to Listen to Wise Counsel

The world tells us to follow our instincts, but Proverbs repeatedly urges us to seek wise counsel. "The way of fools seems right to them, but the wise listen to advice." (Proverbs 12:15)

Godly wisdom often contradicts worldly thinking, and we need the voices of Scripture, godly mentors, and the Holy Spirit to guide us. Proverbs trains us to listen, learn, and walk in the safety of wise instruction, rather than stumbling in the darkness of worldly influence.

Final Thoughts

The Book of Proverbs is more than ancient literature—it is a divine blueprint for wise living in a foolish world. In a culture that constantly pressures us to conform, Proverbs points us back to the unshakable foundation of God's truth. It exposes lies, reveals pitfalls, and equips us to make decisions that lead to life, not destruction. By studying Proverbs, meditating on its truths, and applying its principles, Christians can resist the influence of the world and live lives that are not just smart—but spiritually wise and eternally impactful. If you want to stand strong in a culture of compromise, start by letting the wisdom of Proverbs renew your mind and shape your walk.

Taking Action

Think | Write | Grow

Based on what you learned in this chapter:

What's something you will stop doing or a habit you will break?

_____

_____

What's something you will start doing or a habit you will create?

_____

_____

What's the potential positive impact of improving in this area?

_____

_____

Chapter Forty-Eight

Repent, Believe, and Receive

Rival 7: World Influence

At the heart of the Christian faith stands a single, world-changing truth: Jesus Christ saved us by His work on the cross. No greater act of love has ever been displayed than when the sinless Son of God laid down His life to rescue a broken, sinful humanity. The cross is not just a historical event—it is the centerpiece of redemption, the bridge between a holy God and a fallen world, and the key to living the abundant life God intended for us.

So, what does it mean that Jesus saved us by the cross? And how do we receive that salvation and step into the abundant life He offers?

The Problem: Our Separation from God

From the beginning, God created humanity to walk in close relationship with Him. But sin—our rebellion and disobedience—separated us from God's presence. Romans 3:23 says, "For all have sinned and fall short of the glory of God." No amount of good works, religion, or moral effort can bridge the gap sin creates.

Because God is just, sin demands judgment. But because God is love, He provided a solution: Jesus Christ.

The Solution: Jesus's Work on the Cross

Jesus came into the world fully God and fully man, lived a sinless life, and willingly went to the cross to take our place. On the cross, He bore the full weight of humanity's sin and the judgment it deserved. He paid the penalty we could never pay, offering Himself as the perfect sacrifice.

Isaiah 53:5 says, "But He was pierced for our transgressions, He was crushed for our iniquities; the punishment that brought us peace was upon Him, and by His wounds we are healed."

At the cross:

- Our sins were forgiven.

- Our guilt was removed.

- The power of death was broken.

- Satan's claim on our lives was canceled.

When Jesus cried out, "It is finished" (John 19:30), it wasn't a cry of defeat—it was a declaration of complete victory. The work of salvation was done.

The Invitation: How to Receive Salvation

Salvation is not something we earn—it's a gift we receive by grace through faith. Ephesians 2:8–9 tells us, "For it is by grace you have been saved, through faith—and this is not from yourselves, it is the gift of God—not by works, so that no one can boast."

To be saved, the Bible outlines a simple but life-changing response:

1. Repent: Turn away from sin and turn toward God. Repentance is not just feeling sorry—it's a sincere decision to leave behind the old life.

2. Believe: Trust in Jesus Christ alone as your Savior, believing He died for your sins and rose again. Romans 10:9 says, "If you confess with your mouth, 'Jesus is Lord,' and believe in your heart that God raised Him from the dead, you will be saved."

3. Receive: Accept God's forgiveness and new life by inviting Jesus into your heart. When you do, you are born again—a new creation, washed clean, and adopted into the family of God.

The Result: Life More Abundantly

Salvation is not just about escaping hell or going to heaven someday—it's about living a transformed life right now. Jesus said in John 10:10, "I have come that they may have life, and have it more abundantly."

What does abundant life look like?

- Freedom from sin's grip: You are no longer a slave to guilt, shame, or addiction. In Christ, you are free.

- Peace with God: No more striving or wondering where you stand with Him. Through Jesus, you are fully accepted and loved.

- Purpose and direction: You're not just surviving—you're living with divine purpose and eternal significance.

- Hope for the future: Even in trials, you have unshakable hope, knowing that God is with you and heaven awaits.

This abundant life doesn't mean everything will be perfect—but it does mean that your soul will be anchored in the One who never changes.

Living the Abundant Life Daily

Once you've received salvation, the journey continues. Living abundantly means walking closely with Jesus every day. Here's how:

- Spend time in God's Word: Let Scripture shape your thoughts and guide your actions.

- Pray continually: Talk to God, bring your needs to Him, and listen for His voice.

- Fellowship with other believers: Church and community are vital for growth and encouragement.

- Live obediently: Follow God's commands not to earn His love, but because you already have it.

- Serve others: Use your gifts to impact others and glorify God.

Final Thoughts

Jesus didn't just die to forgive your sins—He died to give you life. A new life. A free life. A full life. His work on the cross paid the price we couldn't pay and opened the door for anyone—no matter their past—to be saved and transformed. If you haven't yet received that gift, today is the perfect day to surrender your heart to Him. And if you have, don't settle for survival—lean into the abundant life Jesus died to give you. Because of the cross, you are loved, forgiven, redeemed, and called to live a life filled with purpose, joy, and everlasting hope.

Taking Action

Think | Write | Grow

Based on what you learned in this chapter:

What's something you will stop doing or a habit you will break?

_____

_____

What's something you will start doing or a habit you will create?

_____

_____

What's the potential positive impact of improving in this area?

_____

_____

Chapter Forty-Nine

Renewing Your Mind Is Essential

Rival 7: World Influence

In Romans 12:2, the Apostle Paul delivers a command that speaks directly to the spiritual struggle Christians face every day: "Do not be conformed to this world, but be transformed by the renewing of your mind." This verse is more than a theological idea—it's a daily call to live differently in a culture that constantly pushes believers to blend in, compromise, and adopt its values. In a world that exalts self over sacrifice, image over integrity, and feelings over truth, Christians are called to resist conformity and pursue transformation.

But how is that possible? The answer lies in the renewing of our minds—a powerful process by which God changes us from the inside out, shaping our thoughts, desires, and behaviors to reflect the life of Christ.

What Does It Mean to "Be Transformed by the Renewing of Your Mind?"

The word "transformed" in this passage comes from the Greek word *metamorphoo*, the root of our English word *metamorphosis*. It refers to a radical, complete change, like a caterpillar turning into a butterfly. Paul isn't talking about surface-level behavior tweaks—he's talking about a deep spiritual transformation that alters how we think, believe, and live.

The "renewing of your mind" is the spiritual process of replacing old, worldly thought patterns with God's truth. It means unlearning the lies of culture, rejecting the influence of the flesh, and aligning your thinking with the Word of God. When your mind is renewed, your life begins to reflect the will, character, and heart of God.

Why the World Wants You to Conform

Paul warns us: "Do not be conformed to this world." The world—meaning the fallen, godless system around us—has a mold that it wants every person to fit into. It pressures us through media, advertising, social norms, and even entertainment to adopt values that are completely opposed to God's design.

The world says:

- "Do what feels right, even if it's wrong."

- "Chase money, status, and pleasure—they define your worth."

- "Truth is whatever you want it to be."

- "God is optional. You are the center of your life."

This pressure to conform is often subtle, but it's relentless. Without intentional resistance, even strong believers can begin to think like the world, speak like the world, and live like the world—while drifting away from Christ without even realizing it.

How Renewing Your Mind Protects You From Worldly Influence

1. It Rewires Your Perspective with God's Truth

Renewing your mind through Scripture replaces lies with truth. The Bible becomes your filter, your compass, and your foundation. When your thoughts are rooted in God's Word, you can recognize falsehood, resist temptation, and see through the shallow promises of culture.

2. It Strengthens Your Identity in Christ

The world tells you to define yourself by what you do, what you have, or how others see you. God tells you that you are a child of God, redeemed, chosen, and loved. Renewing your mind means constantly reminding yourself of who you are in Christ so that the world can't redefine you.

3. It Helps You Discern God's Will

Romans 12:2 ends with a powerful promise: "Then you will be able to test and approve what God's will is—his good, pleasing, and perfect will." As your mind is renewed, you begin to think with clarity and spiritual wisdom. You're not swayed by emotions, trends, or public opinion—you are led by truth.

4. It Keeps You Spiritually Alert

When your mind is set on God's truth, you can recognize subtle compromises and spiritual dangers. You're less likely to fall into moral traps or adopt ungodly attitudes. A renewed mind is a watchful mind—guarded, aware, and grounded in faith.

How to Renew Your Mind

Daily Scripture Intake: Make God's Word a non-negotiable part of your day. Whether through reading, listening, or memorizing, saturate your mind with truth.

Prayerful Reflection: Ask God to expose any lies you've believed and replace them with His truth. Invite the Holy Spirit to guide your thinking and convict your heart when your mindset doesn't align with God.

Choose God-Honoring Inputs: Limit media and entertainment that promote values opposed to Scripture. Fill your mind with worship, sermons, Christian books, and conversations that point you to Christ.

Practice Obedience: Renewal leads to transformation when you act on the truth you learn. Don't just hear God's Word—live it. The more you obey, the stronger your mind becomes in resisting worldly influences.

Final Thoughts

The battle for your soul begins in your mind. The world wants to shape your thinking, but God wants to transform your life. That transformation doesn't happen by accident—it happens when you choose to renew your mind daily, filling it with God's truth, surrendering your thoughts to Him, and walking in obedience. If you want to resist the patterns of this world, you must be anchored in the Word of God. A renewed mind is your greatest weapon against conformity and compromise. It is how you live, not just differently—but victoriously. Be transformed. Be renewed. Be unshakable in a world that never stops trying to pull you away. Let the mind of Christ shape your every thought—and your life will reflect His glory.

Taking Action

Think | Write | Grow

Based on what you learned in this chapter:

What's something you will stop doing or a habit you will break?

_____

_____

What's something you will start doing or a habit you will create?

_____

_____

What's the potential positive impact of improving in this area?

_____

_____

Chapter Fifty

Summary of 7 Rivals of Faith

Conclusion

Here are seven major rivals of our Christian faith—and why identifying them is the first step to overcoming them.

1. Fear: The Faith-Killer

Fear is perhaps the most immediate and common rival of faith. Where fear thrives, faith often dies. Fear causes us to doubt God's promises, hesitate in obedience, and expect the worst instead of trusting His goodness. Jesus repeatedly told His followers, *"Do not be afraid,"* because He knew fear would rob them of peace, courage, and spiritual authority. Fear is not just a feeling—it is a mindset that says, *"God might not come through."* To overcome fear, we must replace it with trust in God's character. 2 Timothy 1:7 reminds us that God has not given us a spirit of fear, but of power, love, and a sound mind.

2. Pride: The Silent Saboteur

Pride convinces us that we don't need God. It places self above submission and opinion above divine truth. Pride blinds us to correction, makes us self-reliant, and closes our hearts to the transforming work of the Holy Spirit. Satan himself fell because of pride (Isaiah 14:13–15), and the same spirit can infect us when we begin to rely on our own wisdom or strength. James 4:6 says, *"God opposes the proud but gives grace to the humble."* To defeat pride, we must embrace humility, confess our dependence on God, and constantly seek His will over our own.

3. Religion: Rules Without Relationship

Religion becomes a rival of faith when it focuses on outward perfor-mance instead of inward transformation. Legalism, traditions, and ritu-als—while not evil in themselves—can replace an authentic relationship with God if we're not careful. Jesus often rebuked the Pharisees not for their lack of knowledge, but for having hardened hearts hidden behind religious appearances (Matthew 23:27). Religion without grace leads to judgment, hypocrisy, and spiritual burnout. Faith thrives in relationship with Christ. True Christianity is about knowing Jesus, walking with Him, and being changed by His Spirit—not merely checking spiritual boxes.

4. Ignorance of God: A Faith Without Foundation

You can't trust a God you don't know. Many Christians struggle with weak faith simply because they don't truly understand who God is—His nature, His promises, and His Word. Hosea 4:6 says, *"My people are de-stroyed for lack of knowledge."* Ignorance leaves us vulnerable to decep-tion, discouragement, and compromise. The antidote is clear, which is to pursue God through Scripture. The more we know Him, the more our faith grows. Knowing God personally deepens our trust and gives us the strength to endure trials.

5. Past Hurts: Pain That Blocks Belief

Unresolved pain—whether from betrayal, loss, disappointment, or trau-ma—can become a rival to our faith when it hardens our hearts or causes us to question God's goodness. Many people walk away from God not be-cause of theology, but because they've experienced real pain and haven't processed it through the lens of faith. They begin to believe the lie: *"If God really loved me, this wouldn't have happened."* But healing comes when we bring our wounds to Christ. Psalm 34:18 promises, *"The Lord is close to the brokenhearted."* Faith often grows strongest when we surrender our pain and trust God to redeem it.

6. Materialism: Trusting Stuff Over the Savior

Materialism tells us that security, happiness, and identity come from what we own, not who we belong to. It's a slow drift from faith in God's provision to dependence on money, possessions, and success. Jesus warned in Matthew 6:24, *"You cannot serve both God and money."* The danger of materialism is that it numbs our spiritual hunger and shifts our priorities from the eternal to the temporary. To fight this rival, we must live with open hands, practice generosity, and keep our eyes fixed on heavenly treasure.

7. World Influence: Conforming Instead of Transforming

The world constantly bombards us with messages, values, and pressures that conflict with God's truth. Whether it's moral compromise, cultural norms, or social expectations, world influence tempts us to blend in rather than stand firm. Romans 12:2 urges us, *"Do not be conformed to the pattern of this world, but be transformed by the renewing of your mind."* When we absorb the world more than the Word, our faith weakens. Staying rooted in Christ, in community, and in Scripture empowers us to resist the sway of culture and remain faithful to God's ways.

Final Thoughts

Each of these rivals—fear, pride, religion, ignorance, past hurts, materialism, and worldly influence—wages war against our faith. Some creep in silently, while others come in like a storm. But the good news is this: God is greater than them all. When we choose to trust, humble ourselves, pursue relationship over ritual, seek to know God deeply, surrender our pain, live with generosity, and resist worldly pressure, our faith becomes strong, resilient, and unshakable. Faith isn't just believing in God—it's choosing Him over everything that tries to replace Him. Guard your faith. Feed it. Fight for it. And you'll find that nothing the enemy throws at you can separate you from the love and power of God.

www.ingramcontent.com/pod-product-compliance
Lightning Source LLC
Chambersburg PA
CBHW051513120626
46551CB00012B/897